DARK RAPTURE

An American
Theater Noir

Eric Overmyer

BROADWAY PLAY PUBLISHING INC
New York
www.broadwayplaypublishing.com
info@broadwayplaypublishing.com

I0139509

DARK RAPTURE
© Copyright 1993 by Eric Overmyer

First printing, this edition: July 2013
I S B N: 978-0-88145-582-3
Book design: Marie Donovan
Word processing: Microsoft Word for Windows
Typographic controls: Xerox Ventura Publisher 2.0 PE
Typeface: Palatino
Printed on recycled acid-free paper and bound in the USA.

for Ellen McElduff

ORIGINAL PRODUCTION

DARK RAPTURE was commissioned by The Empty
Space Theater in Seattle, Kurt Beattie, Artistic Director;
Melissa Hines, Managing Director. The first
performance was on 6 May 1992, with the following
cast and creative contributors:

RAY ....Peter Silbert
BABCOCK/NIZAM .... David Mong
JULIA ....Katie Forgette
LEXINGTON/SCONES .... David Pichette
VEGAS/MATHIS/SCONES ....Robert Wright
TONY/DANNY/LOUNGE SINGER ...... Rex McDowell
RON/WAITER .... Chris Shanahan
RENEE/WAITRESS .... Jessica Marlowe
MAX ....Sally Smythe

Director ....Kurt Beattie
Design/set .... Peggy McDonald
Costumes .... Paul Chi-ming Louey
Lights .... Michael Wellborn
Sound ....David Pascal
Production stage manager .... Becky Barnett

The author wishes to thank Kurt Beattie and Bob
Wright for their support, encouragement, and powers
of persuasion, without which DARK RAPTURE would
not have been written.

The play will be included in Otis Guernsey's BEST
PLAYS OF 1992.

This production was chosen as one of the three best productions outside New York City during the 1992 season by the American Theater Critics Association. A revised version of DARK RAPTURE was presented by New York Stage and Film Company, Producing Directors Mark Linn-Baker, Max Mayer, and Leslie Urdang, at The Powerhouse Theater at Vassar, Poughkeepsie NY (Executive Director, Dixie Sheridan; Producing Director, Beth Fargis-Lancaster). The first performance was on 15 July 1992, with the following cast and creative contributors:

RAY	David Strathairn
BABCOCK/NIZAM	Dan Moran
JULIA	Frances McDormand
LEXINGTON/MATHIS	Jon Tenney
VEGAS/BARTENDER	Larry Joshua
TONY/DANNY	Joseph Siravo
RON/WAITER/SCONES/LOUNGE SINGER	Bruce MacVittie
RENEE/WAITRESS	Marissa Chibas
MAX	Ellen McElduff
Director	Max Mayer
Design/set	Andy Jackness
Costumes	Candice Donnelly
Lights	Don Holder
Sound	Jeremy Grody
Production stage manager	Elise-Ann Konstantin

The author wishes to thank Max Mayer and Leslie Urdang for the NYS&F production, where the version of the play published here took shape under the most congenial of circumstances.

CHARACTERS

RAY
BABCOCK
JULIA
LEXINGTON
VEGAS
TONY
RON
RENEE
MAX (MARGARET)
NIZAM
MATHIS
SCONES
DANNY
LOUNGE SINGER
WAITER *(Cabo)*
BARTENDER *(Seattle)*
WAITRESS *(Key West)*

The play requires six men and three women. RAY, JULIA and MAX should not be doubled. The other actors may be doubled in a number of ways. The actor playing BABCOCK could also play NIZAM. The actor playing LEXINGTON could play MATHIS or SCONES. The actor playing VEGAS could play BARTENDER (Seattle), and SCONES or MATHIS. The actor playing TONY could play DANNY and LOUNGE SINGER. The actor playing RON could play LOUNGE SINGER, SCONES or MATHIS and WAITER (Cabo). The actress playing RENEE should also play WAITRESS (Key West).

Act One
Scene One

(Slide: Northern California. A hillside.)

(Night. A great fire in the distance. Smoke. Gusting reddish light. Sirens. Howling wind. Explosions.)

(RAY appears. He's exhilarated, soaked in sweat and smeared with soot, grinning as he tries to catch his breath.)

(BABCOCK appears out of the darkness. RAY senses his presence, turns, sees him, and nods.)

RAY: Quite a night.

BABCOCK: Fuckin' A. Nothin' spookier 'n a night fire, man. Makes you feel so all alone. I remember. One time. Big Island. Lava flow. Big orange tongues a molten magma whatever creepin' down the hillside like some kinda hellacious glacier. Like some kinda red-hot tectonic taffy. Eerie fuckin' thing to be comin' at ya outa the fuckin' dark, I'm tellin' ya. Fry an egg on that air. That's how hot it was. Softboil one on the palm a your hand. Melt cars. Asphalt like butter. Houses'd just pop. Bang. Like paper bags. Like that.

(He cups his hands and slaps them together, making a popping sound.)

BABCOCK: Kablooee. Spontaneous combust. From the sheer fuckin' heat. Kablam. What can you do but grab the cat, count the kids, and say a prayer to St. Jude the lava runs outa geothermal juice 'fore it dessicates you 'n yours like so much delicatessen jerky. Just sit back 'n watch it comin' toward you. Like sheer fuckin' inevitability. Lurchin' outa the dark rapture.

(Pause. RAY *looks at him, curious, then looks away. A series of explosions in the distance.)*

BABCOCK: See what I mean? Poppin' those fancy houses. Like so many lightbulbs on blacktop.

RAY: Eucalyptus.

BABCOCK: Eucalyptus what? Trees?

RAY: Those explosions. Eucalyptus. The resins. Flammable.

BABCOCK: No shit. Eucalyptus trees. This is some night fire. Never seen nothin' like this. Whoosh.

RAY: I have.

BABCOCK: Bullshit. I mean. Hard to believe. All hell breakin' loose up there 'n flyin' around like pure fuckin' insanity. Full-fledged firestorm. Half the goddamn city's up in flames.

RAY: Cambodia.

BABCOCK: Night fire?

RAY: As a matter of fact.

BABCOCK: I been Cambodia. Interesting place.

(More explosions)

BABCOCK: Fuck me.

RAY: Exciting, isn't it?

BABCOCK: Well, yeah. One word for it. Outa the ordinary.

RAY: I mean, this is what we live for. Catastrophe. Chaos.

BABCOCK: I know what you mean.

RAY: Out of our control. This is what we really want. Deep down. This is where we get our stories. Surviving

catastrophe. What do you think love is? What do you
think romance is all about?

BABCOCK: I always wondered.

RAY: Ongoing twenty-four hour we never close
home-made natural disaster. I mean, you can't always
count on the occasional earthquake to come along just
when you need a jolt of pure adrenaline to jump start
your heart. What I'm saying is, we have a deep-seated
need to manufacture our own inclement weather.

BABCOCK: Hey. Into every life. A little rain must fall.
Am I right?

RAY: Right.

BABCOCK: I was up north in Duckburg when Mt. St.
Helen's shot her wad. Never seen nothin' like that.
A blizzard of dry grey ash. Fallin' and fallin', all night
long. You never heard such a hush. Absolute silence.
Seemed like the end of the world to me.

(Pause. BABCOCK watches the fire rage.)

BABCOCK: Don't know what it is. Cataclysmic natural
disasters just seem to follow me around.

RAY: Used to set the jungle on fire all the time.
Almost couldn't help it. No big deal.

BABCOCK: Well, I guess natural catastrophes are pretty
interesting. If you survive 'em. You got a house up
there?

(RAY looks up the hill into the dark.)

RAY: So far. Looks like.

BABCOCK: Which one?

(RAY points.)

BABCOCK: What the fuck you doin' down here, shootin'
the shit with me?

RAY: Came down to take a look. I wanted to get some distance. Get a vista. This. This is—spectacular.

BABCOCK: Never know. Could get lucky. Wind might change. Could rain. Sometimes the fire jumps. Passes over for no particular reason, moves on to someone else. Like the Angel of Death. Could come through unscathed. Never know. On the other hand. Better grab the family snaps. Take what you need 'n leave the rest.

RAY: I'll do that.

BABCOCK: Quite a night. Fuckin' A.

RAY: Actually, the world seems very peaceful to me, tonight. Quiet.

(BABCOCK *extends his hand.*)

BABCOCK: Name's Babcock.

(RAY *hesitates a moment, then shakes* BABCOCK's *hand.*)

RAY: Pleased to meet you.

BABCOCK: Good luck up there.

RAY: Thanks.

(RAY *leaves.* BABCOCK *watches him go up the hill towards the fire and disappear into the night.*)

BABCOCK: Crazy fuck. Whoosh.

(BABCOCK *disappears.*)

Scene Two

(*Slide: Cabo San Lucas. A hotel room.*)

(*Morning*)

(JULIA, *half-naked on the edge of the bed. Drinks from a bottle of tequila.* DANNY *lies on the bed beside her, eyes closed, motionless.*)

JULIA: Cabo. Tequila. White light. Blue and white light. Blue tiles, white curtains. Blue sky, blue sea. Hot white light. Scraps of white cotton clothing scattered across a blue bed. Straw flowers. Salt. Blue agave. Breeze.

(She drinks. Holds out the bottle. Without opening his eyes or otherwise stirring, DANNY reaches up with one hand, finds the bottle, takes it, drinks.)

JULIA: I thought you were dead.

DANNY: Hmmmmm. Not yet. Couple more days of this.

JULIA: Think of something blue and white.

DANNY: You're drunk.

JULIA: Drinking all day. Drinking before dark. Drinking at dawn. This is a whole other world. This is a whole other way of life. I love this. I can see the attraction. I haven't done this since I was a kid. College. San Francisco. Used to hang out at this little laundromat on Potrero Hill. Get a bottle of gin and watch the dryer go round.

DANNY: Some fun.

JULIA: Some fun. It was, you know. It really was. Gimme.

(She holds out her hand. He gives her the bottle. She drinks.)

JULIA: It's gonna be hot today.

DANNY: It's hot everyday. That's what makes it Mexico.

JULIA: I'm starting to melt. Finally. Stress. Toxins. Melting away. I've been waiting for this. Heat and tequila. Doin' the trick.

(She kisses him.)

JULIA: And sex. Mustn't forget sex.

DANNY: No, no. I wouldn't.

(They kiss.)

JULIA: You could help me. Help me melt.

DANNY: Okay. Do my best. Give it a shot.

(They kiss.)

JULIA: It's gonna be hot. It's gonna be moist.

DANNY: Sticky. Hot and sticky.

JULIA: Juicy. Juicy, not sticky. We're gonna get wet. Very very very wet.

(They kiss.)

JULIA: We're gonna sweat. A lot. We're gonna slip 'n slide. We're gonna be damp all over.

DANNY: Promise?

JULIA: Cross my heart, hope to die.

(They kiss.)

DANNY: Julia.

JULIA: Danny.

(She raises the bottle, looks at the worm.)

JULIA: Dibs on the worm.

DANNY: All yours, baby.

JULIA: Oh, shit. We're outa salt. Oh, what, oh, what, oh what are we gonna do? Wait. Hold everything. I have an idea.

(She leans over. Licks up his breastbone, licks the hollow of his neck. Smiles. Licks her lips.)

JULIA: Salty.

(She drinks.)

JULIA: Ah. Not too shabby. Not too shabby at all.

(He leans over. Licks up her breastbone. Licks the hollow of her neck.)

JULIA: Ooo. Ah.

(He licks the front of her neck. She closes her eyes, clutches his hair. He licks around the base of her neck, licks the back of her neck, behind her ears.)

JULIA: Oh my god. Oh fuck.

(He stops, pulls back, takes the bottle, licks his lips, drinks.)

JULIA: Salty enough for you?

DANNY: Not nearly.

JULIA: I think you know what to do about that, cowboy.

DANNY: I think I do.

(He takes a big swig, but doesn't swallow. They kiss. He opens his mouth. Tequila runs into her mouth, overflows, runs down her neck. They laugh. They fall back on the bed. They kiss.)

Scene Three

(Slide: Northern California. The fire site.)

(Morning. Two men in suits, VEGAS and LEXINGTON, look over the charred landscape of ash and charcoal.)

LEXINGTON: X marks the spot.

VEGAS: Hard to tell.

LEXINGTON: There's the bend in the road. There's the ridge. Over there's where the big white Victorian was.

VEGAS: Sure?

LEXINGTON: Positive.

VEGAS: Kinda hard to get your bearings. In the absence of what was.

LEXINGTON: The white Victorian. Which was next to the craftsman bungalow. Which was next to the newish split-level with the leaky skylights.

VEGAS: How do you know they were leaky?

LEXINGTON: You ever heard a skylights don't leak? Can't be done. The limits of human ingenuity. We cannot keep skylights from leaking. We cannot cure the common cold. And we cannot make a good-tasting spermicidal jelly.

VEGAS: I grew up New York. You know? Always buildin' it up 'n tearin' it down. Once somethin' was gone I could never remember what it was before it wasn't. And once somethin' else went up in its place, forget about it. Walk by one day, everything's fine, like always, walk by the next day, hey, shit, it's gone, this wasn't here yesterday, what did this used to be, remember? Shit. I could never remember.

LEXINGTON: This is their house. The Gaines residence. Ray and Julia's. Where it was. Take my word for it.

VEGAS: We know where Julia is. So, where's Ray?

LEXINGTON: That's one question.

VEGAS: Think he's up here?

LEXINGTON: Possible. They're still digging 'em out. Bits and pieces.

VEGAS: Man, earthquake, flood, fire. The actuarials in this area are gettin' positively apocalyptic. What's next? Famine? I'm thinkin' about movin' somewhere safe.

LEXINGTON: Oh yeah? Somewhere safe? Where would that be?

(Pause. VEGAS shrugs.)

VEGAS: I'll let you know.

LEXINGTON: Radio says body count's twenty-eight. So far. Another fifty-three unaccounted for. Missing.

VEGAS: Including Ray.

LEXINGTON: Including Ray. Figure most a the so-called missing are just outa town.

VEGAS: Business.

LEXINGTON: Business. Yeah. But they're all on their way back home by now. Caught the late clips on CNN, holy cow, there goes the life's savings, the whole enchilada, up in flames, browned out in their bermudas, tossed 'n turned all night, grabbed the first flight out bright and early, throwin' back the bloody Marys and poppin' Prozac, already fillin' out claim forms, cryin' the blues over their BMW's. Couple of 'em are still stuck abroad somewhere, tryin' to get back from Paris. Prague. Constantinople. And some of 'em. Some of 'em are still blissfully unawares as to what's transpired to the old neighborhood. Yuppie scum. Fucked seven ways from Sunday and don't even know it yet. Took off for a long weekend, a little r 'n r, a little illicit extramarital hanky panky. Bahamas. Rosarita Beach.

VEGAS: Cabo San Lucas.

LEXINGTON: Cabo San Lucas. Come home tan, laid, relaxed, got their lies and alibis all lined up like so many ducks, bang bang bang, are they in for a shock.

VEGAS: Could post-facto ruin your whole vacation. In retrospect. Cast a pall.

LEXINGTON: Doesn't do anything for my disposition. So maybe Julia is just tearin' off a piece on the side. Gets back from a little extramarital fuckin' around, finds the house the husband the Mercedes, up in smoke. Let's hope she didn't lose anything didn't belong to her.

VEGAS: We know Ray didn't go to Cabo.

LEXINGTON: That we know.

VEGAS: Babcock had an extended conversation with him.

(BABCOCK *appears.*)

LEXINGTON: Where? Here, at the house?

BABCOCK: Down there on the flat.

LEXINGTON: Fuck was he doin' down there?

BABCOCK: Who knows? Admirin' the view.

LEXINGTON: Sure it was him?

BABCOCK: Fit the description.

LEXINGTON: So you swap lies, trade recipes. Then.

BABCOCK: Then he goes back up the hill, see if the fire's gonna do his house. Guess it did, huh? He went in. He came back out. Carryin' a coupla suitcases.

LEXINGTON: Ah ha.

BABCOCK: Puts 'em down. Goes back in. Then this whole side a the hill goes up. Whoosh. Then I don't see him no more. Then I don't see nothin' no more, on account a the smoke. Then I go home. Call you guys, tell you to come up, maybe we got a problem.

LEXINGTON: So what'd you talk about? You and Ray?

BABCOCK: Natural disasters. Catastrophe theory. Chaos. Cambodia.

LEXINGTON: Cambodia.

BABCOCK: Cambodia. Jungle fires versus conflagrations in a semiwooded urban setting.

(LEXINGTON *sighs, turns to* VEGAS.)

LEXINGTON: So Ray could be up here. Somewhere. Amongst the rubble. Last seen.

VEGAS: Crispy critter.

LEXINGTON: It's possible.

VEGAS: Likely, even.

LEXINGTON: Awful convenient.

VEGAS: He didn't know.

LEXINGTON: Opportunity. Window of.

VEGAS: He wasn't in on it. Assuming there's something to be in on.

LEXINGTON: You know how many people go missing every year? Never come back from that fifteen-minute jaunt around the corner? Go to the market for a quart a milk and vanish into thin? Take the main chance and disappear? Walk away and don't look back?

VEGAS: I dunno. How many?

LEXINGTON: Many. I dunno. A lot. I read. A million.

VEGAS: A million a year?

LEXINGTON: Yeah. Something like that. A million. Roughly. More or less.

VEGAS: I'd say less. I mean, a million a year. Pretty soon that'd add up to nobody left to mind the fuckin' store.

LEXINGTON: Factor in babies.

VEGAS: Factor in dead people.

LEXINGTON: Okay, a lot. Less than a million. Go missing. Take off. Change their names.

BABCOCK: Guys dodgin' child support.

LEXINGTON: Not just. Not only.

VEGAS: I been tempted. Start over.

LEXINGTON: Yeah, sure. Who hasn't? A clean slate. Which takes how long you figure before it gets completely fucked up again like your old life?

VEGAS: Not long.

LEXINGTON: Not long indeed.

VEGAS: Because, like the man said, wherever you go, there you are.

LEXINGTON: Right. So we wait a few days, see if they find Ray Gaines amongst the rubble. They don't, we wait for him to fuck up his brand-new last best chance.

VEGAS: Which he would be bound to do.

LEXINGTON: I feel certain of it.

VEGAS: He didn't know. He had no idea this was his main chance. The door swings open. Hallelujah. He didn't know.

LEXINGTON: Maybe he suspected. Maybe the hairs on the back a his neck stood up.

VEGAS: That happen to you?

LEXINGTON: Yeah. Happen to you?

VEGAS: Yeah. Definitely. Alla time.

LEXINGTON: Babcock. Happen to you?

BABCOCK: Never.

LEXINGTON: How come you're still alive?

BABCOCK: Just lucky, I guess.

LEXINGTON: What about the merry maybe widow?

VEGAS: Julia? Maybe.

LEXINGTON: Maybe she'll come back from Cabo.

VEGAS: If she didn't, that would be a big big clue.

LEXINGTON: Maybe at this moment, the hairs on the back of her neck are standing up.

VEGAS: I wouldn't be surprised. What I hear, everything else was.

(They laugh.)

LEXINGTON: Wonder if Ray knew about that? His wife and Danny. The stuntman.

VEGAS: Hey. Modern marriage.

LEXINGTON: Babcock. Ever been to Cabo?

BABCOCK: Baja? Sure. Tuna fishing.

LEXINGTON: Bring me back a can.

(BABCOCK nods, leaves.)

VEGAS: Cabo. Wonder she's still there.

LEXINGTON: See how she takes the news when she gets back.

VEGAS: If she gets back.

LEXINGTON: Like you say. That would be a big big clue.

(It starts to rain.)

VEGAS: Startin' to rain. Shit.

LEXINGTON: Let's get the hell outa here before the whole hillside slides into the Bay.

VEGAS: Life's little mysteries.

(They go. The sound of the rain intensifies.)

Scene Four

(Slide: Los Angeles. A used car lot.)

(Night. Vapor lights. Wet pavement gleams. Plastic pennants. Two young men, TONY and RON, stand smoking cigarettes. A middle-aged salesman, NIZAM, approaches them, all smiles.)

NIZAM: How can I help you?

TONY: Looks like you had some rain.

NIZAM: Yeah. Cloudburst. Didn't last long.

RON: Could use it up north.

NIZAM: I heard. Terrible, terrible. What a tragedy.

TONY: They know, was it arson?

NIZAM: I don't know. I don't know. Do they know? Has it been on the news? I don't think they know yet.

RON: Had to be arson.

TONY: Why?

RON: So big.

NIZAM: Not necessarily. The drought's been worse up
north than here, even. Terrible.

TONY: Really.

NIZAM: Oh, my, yes. Awful. Whole municipalities
running out of water.

RON: We're not from around here.

NIZAM: Desalinization plants. That's what they're
building up north. That's the future. If I were your age.
That's what I'd get into.

TONY: Desalinization.

NIZAM: Yes. A goldmine.

RON: Sounds exciting.

TONY: Like the Middle East. Right?

NIZAM: I don't know.

TONY: Kuwait. Didn't the Iraqis?

NIZAM: Yes, I think so.

RON: Pumped oil into their desalinization plant.

TONY: Fucked up their drinking water.

NIZAM: I seem to recall that.

TONY: You look like you're from the Middle East.

NIZAM: Los Angeles.

RON: We're from Detroit.

TONY: The Motor City.

RON: Why we're here. Wheels.

NIZAM: So. You are thinking about buying a car?

RON: Oh, we're gonna buy us a car.

TONY: Why we're here. Tony—

NIZAM: Pleased to meet you.

RON: Ron—

(They shake.)

NIZAM: I am Nizam.

TONY: Nizam. Sounds Middle Eastern.

RON: Tony, give the man a break. He already told you.

NIZAM: Yes. I am American.

TONY: Yeah. Just asking. You know. Roots. Background. Ethnic heritage. Which chip of the glorious mosaic. Sounds Middle Eastern. Nizam. You know, like Tony, that's Italian or something.

RON: You're not Italian.

TONY: My point. Like in Detroit, a lotta people from the Middle East. You know. Chaldeans. Lebanese.

NIZAM: I am American.

TONY: I understand that. Just wondering about your name. Nizam. What kind of name is Nizam? That's all.

NIZAM: I don't know. What kind of car are you thinking about?

RON: Good shape. Good mileage. Oil tight. Never been in a bad wreck. Odometer hasn't turned over.

TONY: In short. The impossible dream, huh?

NIZAM: Not at all. We have a number of vehicles that fit that description. May I show them to you?

(He starts off. RON follows. TONY doesn't move. NIZAM and RON stop, look at TONY.)

RON: You comin'?

TONY: Don't think so.

RON: What's the problem?

TONY: Let's go somewhere else.

RON: Long as we're here.

TONY: I don't like the vibe.

NIZAM: I thought you were interested in buying a car.

RON: We are.

NIZAM: I did not mean to insult you. Please accept my apologies.

TONY: I was only making conversation.

NIZAM: My fault. I am sensitive about my name.

TONY: No, I was bein' nosey. None of my business.

NIZAM: Okay. No problem. Okay?

TONY: Okay.

NIZAM: Good.

(He starts off again. TONY *doesn't budge.* NIZAM *stops.)*

TONY: I'd still like to know. I mean. Let's establish a little trust here. This is a fraught situation. Used cars. I like you call 'em used cars, by the way. Not pre-owned or some such bullshit.

NIZAM: Well. There is no need for such subterfuge, is there?

(Pause)

NIZAM: People have stereotypes. I'm sure you understand.

TONY: They make assumptions.

NIZAM: Exactly so.

RON: People are prejudiced.

NIZAM: Undoubtedly I am oversensitive.

TONY: No, no, not at all. Ron and me, we know what you mean. We get that all the time. Wise guys. Goombahs. Guidos. Greaseballs. Guinea fucks.

NIZAM: I thought you said you were not Italian.

TONY: My point. What is it people call us?

RON: When they find out our ethnic point of origin?

TONY: Exactly.

RON: Rug merchants.

TONY: Rug merchants. You ever heard that one, Nizam?

NIZAM: No. What is that? Lebanese?

TONY: I'm surprised you never heard that, Nizam. A person of your particular ethnicity.

NIZAM: I'm not an Arab. I told you.

TONY: I didn't say you were a rag head. Towel head. Camel jockey. Nizam. Nizam. I don't know. Sounds Turkish to me. What do you think, Ron?

RON: Nizam? Turkish. Definitely.

NIZAM: I don't understand. I thought you were interested in buying a car.

TONY: Oh, we're gonna buy us a car.

(Pause)

NIZAM: Who are you?

RON: Just a couple of rug merchants from Detroit.

TONY: You never heard that one, Nizam? Rug merchants. Armenians.

(Pause)

NIZAM: I don't have a quarrel with you, my friends.

(Pause)

NIZAM: Stupid, really. I always meant to change it. George. I like George. My parents.

(Pause)

NIZAM: I always wanted an American name. I was born here. L.A. East Hollywood. Western and Santa Monica. An Armenian neighborhood.

(Pause. Smiles.)

NIZAM: Please, my friends. I'm sorry. I should have just told you. Let us go look at some cars. Yes?

(He takes a step toward the lot. TONY *draws a gun.* NIZAM *stops.)*

NIZAM: Please. I have a family.

TONY: Give me your wallet.

NIZAM: Tell your friend not to shoot me.

RON: He has a mind of his own. Better do as he says.

*(*NIZAM *hands* TONY *his wallet.)*

TONY: Kneel.

*(*NIZAM *kneels.)*

NIZAM: There's money in the office safe. You can have that.

TONY: Speaking of prejudice. How do you feel about rug merchants? Deep down.

NIZAM: I would never use that term.

TONY: Armenian Holocaust?

NIZAM: Terrible.

TONY: Did it or did it not occur?

NIZAM: I don't know. Ancient history. Probably.

TONY: Probably?

NIZAM: I had nothing to do with that. I am an American. I was born in Los Angeles.

TONY: You keep saying that. Like it made a difference. The Turkish government says the Armenian Holocaust never happened. The Turkish government says although it never happened, even so, the Armenians brought whatever didn't ever happen on themselves. A few people died. Unfortunate. Wartime. The odd atrocity. Can't be helped. Regrettable. But nothin' like the more than one and a half million Armenian dead. Is that your position? In the ballpark?

NIZAM: I am an American citizen. I know nothing about that issue.

TONY: That issue? That issue?

(TONY has been looking through NIZAM's wallet. Now he pulls out a card.)

TONY: I would think the Honorary Turkish Vice-Consul to the City of Los Angeles would tend to agree with his government on that issue.

NIZAM: An honorary position. Ceremonial. Not political. I just help people. You know. Visa problems. Translators.

TONY: Okay.

(He puts the gun away.)

TONY: You can get up now.

(NIZAM gets up, slowly. Pause.)

RON: Sorry.

(TONY hands NIZAM his wallet.)

NIZAM: Thank you.

RON: You speak Turkish?

NIZAM: No.

RON: Too bad. Your parents, right? Mine, too. They never spoke Armenian at home. Never wanted us to learn, wanted us to be American.

(NIZAM doesn't answer. Pause.)

RON: East Hollywood. I got cousins, East Hollywood.

(Pause)

RON: My Dad. My Dad always said. The terrible thing was. We were brothers. Us and the Turks. We lived together. He'd get real quiet. His eyes would get very big and dark. Whole thing really tore him up.

(Pause)

TONY: So. About this car.

NIZAM: You still want to see a car?

TONY: Why we're here. Wheels.

NIZAM: I think you should go now. Get the fuck out.

(Pause)

RON: C'mon, Tony. Man's upset. Can't blame him.
Little outa line.

TONY: Wait wait wait. What is your feeling about this?
Now that we're not chatting at gunpoint. Speak freely.
Nizam. I'd really like to know.

NIZAM: About what? The Armenian Question?

TONY: Yeah. The Armenian Question. That issue.
That ancient history.

NIZAM: All that happened a long time ago. Nineteen,
what?

TONY: Fifteen, sixteen, seventeen, eighteen, nineteen—

NIZAM: A long time ago. Before I was born. Before my
father was born. In Turkey. It doesn't matter to me.

TONY: It matters to us.

NIZAM: I understand.

TONY: But did it happen? Do you believe it happened?
That's what I want to know.

NIZAM: I'm sure something terrible happened. Terrible
things happened. I'm sorry.

TONY: I'm not looking for an apology.

NIZAM: Okay.

TONY: I'm looking for acknowledgment. That's all.
Admission of guilt. What the Germans did to the
Gypsies and the Jews. What the Japanese did to the
Chinese and the Koreans. What the Americans did to

the blacks and the Indians. The truth of what happened.
That what happened happened.

NIZAM: I understand. I know how you feel.

TONY: Do you.

NIZAM: You think some great injury was done your
grandparents. Great-grandparents. By mine. You want
retribution. Like the blacks. Reparations for slavery.
But the slaves are all dead. And so are the slave owners.
The living don't know. Who did what to who. So long
ago. It has nothing to do with us. We weren't there.

(Pause)

TONY: History is a living wound.

NIZAM: Listen. I don't know what my great-
grandparents did to yours. Probably nothing. I haven't
done anything to you. I won't pay reparations. Not to
you. Not to the blacks. I didn't own any slaves. I didn't
kill any Armenians. I don't know anyone who did.

(Pause)

TONY: That sound like an unequivocal admission of
historical culpability to you?

(Pause)

RON: No.

TONY: Me either.

*(TONY pulls his gun and fires, shooting NIZAM in the throat.
NIZAM falls, flops, lies still. TONY stands, looking at the
body. Blood begins to spread over the pavement.)*

RON: C'mon. Let's go pick out a car.

*(RON walks off. TONY puts his gun away, walks over and
spits on NIZAM, and walks off.)*

Scene Five

(Slide: Seattle/Cabo San Lucas)

(Late afternoon. Simultaneously.)

(A chic expresso bar in Seattle. Deserted. Rain. A steady downpour. RAY *sits, nursing a cappuccino and looking out at the rain. And:)*

(An open-air thatched-roof bar/restaurant in Cabo San Lucas. Sun. Sounds of birds. DANNY *and* JULIA *are eating, drinking cans of Tecate.)*

RAY: This is it, huh? Famous Seattle rain. Like this all the time?

BARTENDER: What's your name?

RAY: Ray.

BARTENDER: Where you from, Ray?

RAY: California.

BARTENDER: Ever been here before?

RAY: Never.

BARTENDER: You know that expression? Put it where the sun don't shine? They were talkin' about Seattle.

RAY: Relax. I'm not up here to drive up the real estate market, congest traffic, keep the salmon from spawning, or otherwise Californicate Seattle. Really.

BARTENDER: You know, we have a lot of expressions here. California stop. California driver. California consciousness.

RAY: Hey. I come in peace. Honest.

BARTENDER: I'll be the judge of that. So what brings you to paradise? If not to fuck it up?

RAY: Vacation. Thought I'd get outa town 'til my local NPR station finishes its annual pledge drive.

BARTENDER: God, I hate that. Yak yak yak. I'd subscribe already if they'd just shut the fuck up. 'Nother cappuccino?

RAY: Why not?

(BARTENDER *moves off.* JULIA *sighs and stretches.*)

JULIA: Nice. I love it here.

DANNY: Yeah. I'm not used to dining al fresco en Mexico. How do you keep the birds from shitting in your enchiladas?

JULIA: Hunker over your plate.

DANNY: Then they shit in your hair.

JULIA: Life is choices, babe. I could just stay here forever.

DANNY: You'd get so bored in a week.

JULIA: We haven't even done everything on our wish list yet.

(*They kiss.* BARTENDER *brings* RAY *another cappuccino.*)

BARTENDER: (*Re: rain*) Picked a great weekend.

RAY: I thought you said it was like this all the time.

BARTENDER: Promise me you won't move here. I'll slip you a copy of the secret sunshine schedule.

RAY: Secret sunshine schedule.

BARTENDER: Kinda like the *Farmer's Almanac*. Closely guarded secret. Gotta be a native to get one.

RAY: Like you.

BARTENDER: Fuck, no, I'm from Cleveland.

(*He moves off.* DANNY *and* JULIA *break their kiss.*)

JULIA: You've just given me several new ideas for this afternoon's siesta.

DANNY: I was wondering.

JULIA: What?

DANNY: About your husband.

JULIA: Oh, shit.

DANNY: Sorry.

JULIA: Last thing I want to talk about.

DANNY: Forget it.

JULIA: What?

DANNY: Just. What does he think?

JULIA: I don't know.

DANNY: No phone calls, no letters.

JULIA: There aren't any phones. The Mexican mail. That's why we're here. Cabo. That special magic.

DANNY: What does he think you're doing?

JULIA: He trusts me.

DANNY: That's good.

JULIA: He's a trusting soul.

DANNY: Just wondering.

JULIA: Why?

DANNY: I don't have a clear picture of him, that's all. Ray. El Rey. Ex-Ray. El Ray-o ex.

JULIA: Nice guy.

DANNY: Trusts you.

JULIA: Yeah.

DANNY: What is it he does? You told me, I forgot.

JULIA: What does he do or what does he wanna do?

DANNY: Both.

JULIA: He teaches an extension course at State. He wants to be a writer.

DANNY: Really.

JULIA: Screenwriter.

DANNY: Really. How unusual.

JULIA: He does some word processing for a big law firm downtown.

DANNY: Any good?

JULIA: Dynamite. Dynamite word processor.

DANNY: Screenwriter.

JULIA: I don't know. Okay. Maybe. Has promise. I can't tell. I'm not objective. Mostly he lives off my trust fund.

DANNY: And wants to be in show business. Like you.

JULIA: Like me. The difference is—

DANNY: Yes?

JULIA: I'll do it. I will. No question.

DANNY: I'm sure. I have no doubts.

(Pause)

DANNY: Would you hire him? Write your first film? Give him a shot?

JULIA: No.

DANNY: That's cold. Your own wife the producer. Can't catch a break.

JULIA: I don't believe in nepotism.

DANNY: You'd hire me. I'd do your stunts.

JULIA: I'd hire you to body double the leading man. The nude scenes. Get your buns on film. Make you famous.

DANNY: I started as a focus puller. I could pull your focus.

JULIA: Anytime. Please. Please pull my focus. Please.

DANNY: Anytime.

(They kiss. A woman, RENEE, comes into the espresso bar. Sits near RAY. Catches his eye. Smiles.)

RENEE: Wet enough for you?

RAY: Must say that a lot here. Must be one of the favorite local sayings. Like the one about moss growing on your north side.

RENEE: I wouldn't know. I'm from Tampa.

RAY: Spanish moss.

RENEE: Kudzu.

RAY: All that sunshine and kudzu started to get to you, didn't it?

RENEE: I needed a break. A change.

RAY: I know what you mean. Too much of a good thing can drive a man insane.

RENEE: Woman, too.

(BARTENDER *comes over.* RENEE *peruses the menu.*)

BARTENDER: Hey. Local Seattle joke. How much is a Scandinavian haircut? Four dollars. A dollar a side. Guess you have to be a native to appreciate the contours of that particular joke. What'll you have?

RENEE: What's a decaf doppio mocha macchiato?

BARTENDER: Specialty of the house. Absolutely delicious.

RENEE: Absolutely not. Cafe con leche, please.

BARTENDER: Hey, Spanish is the loving tongue. Latte. Unleaded or regular?

RENEE: Regular. No question. Leaded. Extra lead.

BARTENDER: Maximum butter fat?

RENEE: With a spoon.

BARTENDER: Alright.

(BARTENDER *moves off.* BABCOCK *enters the Cabo cafe, sits, watches* DANNY *and* JULIA *neck.*)

RENEE: I've never seen so many expresso bars.
Per capita.

RAY: Crazy for caffeine. Whole town's wired for sound.

RENEE: I guess that's one way to cope with the rain.

RAY: I can think of others.

RENEE: Me, too.

(DANNY and JULIA break their kiss.)

DANNY: Gonna have to spend more time in L.A.

JULIA: I already am.

DANNY: I spend a lot of time in L.A. I live there.

JULIA: I noticed.

(Pause)

DANNY: Does he know?

JULIA: No.

DANNY: He doesn't know what you do in L.A.?

JULIA: He knows I'm putting together a deal. He doesn't
know what I do. Who I do.

*(She kisses him. BABCOCK looks around for a waiter.
WAITER approaches.)*

WAITER: Si, señor.

BABCOCK: Tecate, por favor.

WAITER: Si, señor.

*(WAITER follows BABCOCK's gaze. DANNY and JULIA,
getting hot and heavy.)*

WAITER: No hay problema. Están casados.

BABCOCK: Si. Pero no uno con la otra.

*(WAITER walks off. DANNY and JULIA get up and leave.
BARTENDER brings RENEE's latte.)*

BARTENDER: There you go. A big steaming cup
of high-octane, cholesterol-rich, artery-clogging,

keep-you-up-all-night-staring-at-the-ceiling-
grinding-your-teeth heaven. Enjoy.

(He leaves.)

RENEE: Cheers.

RAY: Salud.

(They clink cups. They drink. A long look.)

RENEE: My name's Renee Valenzuela.

RAY: Spanish.

RENEE: Cuban, actually.

(A pause. She looks at him, expectantly. He decides.)

RAY: Ray. Ray Avila.

RENEE: Avila. Sounds Cuban.

RAY: Czech. Neruda. Neruda was a Czech name.

RENEE: Who's Neruda?

RAY: A poet.

RENEE: A Czech poet.

RAY: A Spanish poet. Chilean, actually.

RENEE: Oh.

(She smiles.)

RENEE: Ray. So, Ray. Tell me about yourself.

(He smiles.)

Scene Six

(Slide: San Francisco. Law offices of Mathis and Scones.)

(Morning. JULIA, *dressed in a sober suit, sits across from* MATHIS, *who opens a briefcase and extracts a stack of papers.)*

MATHIS: I'm sorry this has taken so long, Mrs. Gaines.
My apologies. Profuse.

JULIA: That's quite all right, Mr. Mathis.

MATHIS: We appreciate your patience. We are inundated at the moment. The fire. You can imagine. A veritable tsunami of claims. And the percentage of fraudulent claims. Distressingly high.

JULIA: Really.

MATHIS: Shocking. People exploiting their personal calamity for larcenous remuneration. Imagine. We're seeing some preposterous inflations.

JULIA: Really.

MATHIS: Oh, my, yes. Very creative. Stupid, some of them. Demonstrably false. I mean, would you put in a claim for a painting which is already hanging in at least one major museum? Please. That's why your claim is such a pleasure—well, not a pleasure, of course—

JULIA: It's all right. I know what you mean.

MATHIS: But straightforward. Honest. Well-documented.

JULIA: Yes. Well. I never imagined. You take precautions, but you never imagine. Funny. There were things in the safe deposit box that surprised me. Some silly mementos of our honeymoon. Seashells. I didn't think Ray was so. I don't know. Sentimental. And then there were things missing. Things I expected to find. Photo album. His passport. His lucky Buddha. He never travelled without his lucky Buddha. For a crazy moment I thought, maybe he isn't dead. Maybe he's just gone somewhere. He'll come back.

(Pause)

MATHIS: Where would he go?

JULIA: I don't know.

(Pause)

JULIA: I suppose they were just lying around the house somewhere. Lost in the fire.

(The door opens. SCONES *enters, with a folder.)*

MATHIS: Ah. Here he is.

SCONES: Julia.

JULIA: Mr. Scones.

SCONES: How are you?

JULIA: Holding up. Quite a shock.

SCONES: I should imagine.

(Pause)

JULIA: I was in Cabo. I came down to breakfast. Saw the paper. The headlines. Two days old. And then I couldn't get a seat on a plane back. And then when I got home. And saw the house. Where the house had been. You just can't imagine. You can't conceive of this magnitude of misfortune. Always to others. Never to me.

(Pause)

JULIA: And then when they found the body. What was left of the body. His wedding ring, melted from the heat of the fire. Fused with bone. Not even enough for an urn. Some bone dust, some fragments, the melted ring. All it amounted to in the end was a small ornamental box. Carved. Hardwood. I held it in my hand. I shook it. It rattled and shushed.

(Pause)

MATHIS: I understand the service was quite elegant.

JULIA: Lovely. All his friends. His favorite Bach.

SCONES: It was beautiful.

JULIA: Very nice of you to come.

SCONES: We thought the firm should be represented. And I knew Ray slightly. Mutual friends. The Aragons. We played racquetball once or twice.

(SCONES *opens his folder. Takes out two checks, and some papers, glances at them briefly and passes them across to* JULIA.)

SCONES: The first is for the house, the second is the life insurance payment. Accidental death. Totaling, less our fees and expenses, one point one million dollars. Please sign at the red x's and initial within the circles.

(JULIA *signs.*)

MATHIS: Will you be rebuilding?

JULIA: No. I'm selling the property. Moving to Los Angeles. I have business interests there.

SCONES: Starting over. Starting a new life.

MATHIS: It's best. It's the best thing.

JULIA: Yes.

SCONES: Well. If there's anything further we can do. Please don't hesitate to call.

JULIA: Thank you. Mr. Scones. Mr. Mathis.

(JULIA *pockets the checks. Stands.*)

JULIA: Goodbye, gentlemen. I'm sure I'll never see either of you ever again.

(*She leaves.*)

Scene Seven

(*Slide: Seattle. A hotel room.*)

(*Evening. The sound of a constant, steady rain drumming against the window.* RENEE *is in bed.*)

RENEE: My great-grandfather worked in the cigar factories in Ybor City. The Cuban quarter of Tampa.

With Jose Marti himself. Then when Marti went back to
Cuba to fight for independence, my great-grandfather
followed him. So there was this link with Tampa and
my family that goes way back. So when my parents left
Cuba after Castro, they moved to Tampa instead of
Miami, because of what my Dad heard from his
grandfather.

(RAY *appears in the doorway from the bathroom, wearing
only a towel and brushing his teeth.*)

RENEE: My great-grandfather never touched a tobacco
leaf in his life. He didn't even smoke. He was a reader.
He read out loud while they worked. Rolling cigars.
Newspapers. Pamphlets. Socialist tracts. Revolutionary
stuff. Fairy tales. Novels by Balzac. The workers
demanded a reader. And the owners paid. They
thought it would improve productivity. The owners
didn't care. It was all in Spanish. And the Cubans were
all going back to Cuba as soon as they could. Didn't
have anything to do with Ybor City. With America.

(*Pause*)

RENEE: My dad was a big man. Big hands. He never
talked politics. Which was unusual. I mean, my uncles.
Whenever they started, Castro this, Castro that, he'd
just sit and stare. Like he was a million miles away.
Back in Cuba, maybe.

(*Pause*)

RENEE: I came home from college one spring to check
on him. My mom had died the year before. It was late.
Ten o'clock. He was sitting at the table in his
undershirt. It was hot already. He was sweating.
He was eating yucca, drinking rum. I could smell
the garlic from the street. Through the screendoor.

(*Pause*)

RENEE: I like yucca. Reminds me of my dad. So there
he was. Eating yucca, drinking rum, watching TV.

The local news. Haitians, boat people, down in Miami.
Complaining about the preferential treatment for
Cuban refugees. And my dad's kinda drunk.
And he starts in on what I call the Cuban catechism.
The catalogue of sorrows and betrayals. Marti. Batista.
Castro. Exile in America. Bahia de Cochinos. Bay of
Pigs. And I asked him. Were you in the Bay of Pigs?
I'd never asked him that before. And he said no.
He was in the second wave. Which never happened.
Stuck in Miami. Waiting to go in. Attack Havana.
Take back the casinos. And then he started talking
about Kennedy. The betrayal. He promised them.
He sold them out. He made a deal with the
Communists. I never heard my father like that.
So bitter. From the heart. Hate from the heart.

(Pause)

RENEE: And then he said, I never told anyone this.
Not even your mother. And I said, Popi you can tell me.
And he said, I know who killed him.

(Pause)

RAY: Kennedy.

RENEE: Kennedy.

(Pause)

RAY: So. Did he tell you?

RENEE: Yeah. He made me swear first. Which I did.
On my mother's memory.

(Pause)

RAY: You're not gonna tell me?

(She smiles and shrugs.)

RAY: You know who killed Kennedy? And you're not
gonna tell me?

RENEE: I swore.

RAY: Well, that's an interesting story, Renee. A little frustrating.

(Pause)

RAY: It lacks an ending. It's a bit of a tease, if you know what I mean.

(Pause)

RAY: You know the answer to the greatest mystery of the twentieth century, and you're not gonna tell me? Renee. I thought we had a nice time. Didn't we have a nice time?

RENEE: Yummy. Better than fried yucca.

RAY: That good? So, tell me.

(Pause)

RENEE: He's dead now. Popi. I guess it doesn't matter.

(Pause)

RENEE: He did.

RAY: Who?

RENEE: My father. My father killed Kennedy.

RAY: Your father.

RENEE: Was the second gunman on the grassy knoll.

RAY: He told you that.

RENEE: Yeah. That's what he said. The second gunman. The grassy knoll. They started calling it that later. He didn't know it was the grassy knoll then. He was just there. He fired the second shot. The one that killed him. The one that blew his head apart.

RAY: What else did he tell you?

RENEE: Nothing.

RAY: No details? No context? No plot?

RENEE: No.

RAY: Other Cuban exiles?

RENEE: I assume.

RAY: Who he was working for?

RENEE: Oh. CIA. Obviously. Goes without saying.

RAY: Oh, sure. Well. It'd better. If you know what's good for you. Wait. Your father told you he killed Kennedy. You believed him?

RENEE: Wild, isn't it? I mean, my Daddy killed the President? Popi? But then I started to think about it. I mean, somebody had to do it. I mean, it had to be somebody. Somebody did do it. And why shouldn't that somebody have a family and a daughter? Why shouldn't that somebody be my father? Yeah. I believe he did. No question. He never lied to me. Not once in my whole life.

RAY: But. How do you feel about it? Daddy killed the president?

RENEE: He was my father.

(Pause)

RENEE: So, you see. If my great-grandfather hadn't gone into exile in Tampa with Jose Marti, maybe we wouldn't've come back to this country, and my father wouldn't've killed Kennedy. You can just never tell where a thing gets started, can you?

(RAY nods, goes back into bathroom to rinse out his mouth. RENEE reaches over, turns out the light. RAY re-enters the room in the dark. Gets into bed.)

RAY: What about Oswald?

RENEE: He didn't say.

RAY: Renee—

RENEE: He didn't say. I forgot to ask.

(Pause. RAY turns the light on. Looks at her.)

RENEE: I wasn't thinking clearly.

(He turns the light out. Pause.)

RAY: I'm in bed with a woman whose father killed Kennedy. Told her he killed Kennedy. What am I supposed to feel? I'm not clear what I'm supposed to feel.

RENEE: Feel this.

(Pause)

RAY: That feels nice.

RENEE: Oh. Yes.

(The sound of RAY *and* RENEE *rolling off the bed and hitting the floor. Pause.)*

RAY: Don't stop.

RENEE: I can't see a fuckin' thing. Oh. There we go.

RAY: Right.

(They continue in the dark.)

Scene Eight

(Slide: Santa Barbara. A greenhouse.)

(Afternoon. Rows and rows of orchids. JULIA *is waiting. She paces a little. Sighs. Footsteps on wooden boards. She gets very still. They come nearer. Nearer. She tenses, almost holding her breath.* BABCOCK *appears. She relaxes. Glances at him briefly, then looks away. He stands and watches her until she looks back at him. She frowns.)*

JULIA: I know you.

BABCOCK: Doubt it.

(He walks off. Distracted, JULIA *takes a pack of cigarettes out of her purse, extracts one, and lights up. Takes a drag. A smoke alarm bleats. She jumps.)*

JULIA: Jesus.

(She grinds out the cigarette under her heel. The alarm stops.
LEXINGTON *and* VEGAS *appear behind her. Sensing their*
presence, she turns, sees them, starts again.)

JULIA: Oh. Mr. Lexington. Mr. Vegas. You frightened
me.

VEGAS: Us?

JULIA: You.

LEXINGTON: Shouldn't smoke in here.

JULIA: Forgot where I was. You're late.

VEGAS: God, it's sexy in here. So sexy. Must be the heat,
huh? So damp. Sultry. All this perfume. Hothouse,
huh? These flowers are. They're obscene. Orchids.
Look like sex. Like female genitalia. Don't they? Julia?

JULIA: Yeah. That's what they look like. Pussies.

LEXINGTON: So. How ya doin', Julia?

JULIA: I've been better.

VEGAS: Did we express our condolences?

JULIA: No.

LEXINGTON: Forgive us. We've been remiss.

JULIA: Thank you.

VEGAS: The loss of your husband. A hard thing.

JULIA: Yes.

LEXINGTON: You were close.

JULIA: We were married.

LEXINGTON: Leaves us with a problem, though.
Apparently.

JULIA: The money.

VEGAS: Isn't that always the problem? These situations?

JULIA: Bad luck.

(Pause)

JULIA: I don't know what to do.

LEXINGTON: This is a problem.

VEGAS: Maybe we can help.

LEXINGTON: Tell us where the money is.

JULIA: What do you mean? You know where the money is. It's gone.

VEGAS: Not gone. Missing.

JULIA: It was in the house. It burned up in the fucking fire.

VEGAS: That fire was somethin', you know? I personally know eight mid- to high- level dealers, down dudes, lost homes in that fire. Those guys. Pounds of money. Acres of cash. Big burlap bags of swag in the basement. Enough loose scratch up there to put a dent in the national debt. So much cigarette ash. Tragic.

LEXINGTON: We too have our financial anxieties. You may not realize. Cash flow. Payroll.

VEGAS: Not taxes, thank God.

LEXINGTON: No. Not taxes. We don't pay taxes. We do pay tribute. Contrary to what you may think we are not at the top of the fuckin' food chain. Far from it. Plus, the precedent. Heinous. We can't just let this go. We can't just chalk it up to a so-called act of God and write it off. We'd be outa business in a week.

(Pause)

LEXINGTON: What I wanna know is. Why was our money in your house? Isn't this the crux? The very essence of the matter? Why we're havin' this little chat? *(Inhales)* Perfume. Sheer perfume.

VEGAS: Nectar.

LEXINGTON: Pleasant surroundings. An unexpected perk.

VEGAS: I never been to Santa Barbara before. Nice. Doesn't Reagan live around here somewhere?

LEXINGTON: Still. I'd like to get back to L.A. before dark.

JULIA: The paperwork wasn't in place.

LEXINGTON: You're kidding.

JULIA: I've been constructing a plausible scenario. Hong Kong investors. Capital flight. Large amounts of insecure cash seeking fiduciary sanctuary. Until everything was in place I couldn't deposit that much unlaundered money without risking exposure. Putting our arrangement in jeopardy.

LEXINGTON: Everything was in place. You assured us. Partner.

JULIA: Last minute offshore snafu.

VEGAS: Somebody's brother-in-law in the Caymans needed help with his daughter's orthodonture.

JULIA: Something like that. I was set to make the initial deposit first thing that morning. The day after the fire. Bad luck.

LEXINGTON: The day after the fire.

JULIA: Yes.

LEXINGTON: You were in Cabo. With Danny.

(Pause)

LEXINGTON: How were you supposed to make the fuckin' deposit from Cabo?

JULIA: Ray.

VEGAS: I told you.

LEXINGTON: No, you didn't. Don't start with me.

JULIA: Per my instructions. Prearrangements.

VEGAS: You wouldn't want to share those prearrangements with us.

JULIA: Our deal was, the details are my affair.

VEGAS: So to speak.

LEXINGTON: Our deal was, the money washes through the Caymans' account, less your split. No sign of it, last time I looked. Not a red fucking cent.

(Pause)

VEGAS: Ray.

JULIA: He didn't know. He trusted me.

LEXINGTON: He trusted you? He trusted you? You're in Cabo, fucking some stunt man. Oh, by the way, honey, while I'm in Baja, boffing my boyfriend, could you please run this seven million dollars in small unmarked bills down to this crooked banker friend of mine. He's gonna launder 'em for me at the local fluff n' fold. Don't ask any questions, I'll explain the whole thing when I get back.

JULIA: The parcel was sealed. He had no idea.

VEGAS: A trusting soul, this Ray.

JULIA: Yes.

(Pause)

JULIA: How did you know? About Cabo? About me and Danny?

(They shrug.)

JULIA: That guy who walked through here. I have seen him before. In a cafe in Cabo.

VEGAS: Fuckin' Babcock, huh? 'Bout as inconspicuous as a tarantula on a slice of angel food cake.

LEXINGTON: That's good. You make that up?

VEGAS: Raymond Chandler.

LEXINGTON: I don't know him. Sounds like a smart cookie. Could he maybe replace Babcock.

VEGAS: He's dead.

LEXINGTON: Too bad. Sounds like the kinda guy with whom you could go to the track. Entertaining. So. Julia. To return to the crux.

JULIA: I'll pay you back.

LEXINGTON: Goes without saying.

VEGAS: But how?

LEXINGTON: You don't have our investment. Without which you don't have your production company. And our arrangement is. What's the word? Moot.

VEGAS: Too bad. We were looking forward. A long-term arrangement. Convenient and profitable for both parties. A little glamour. Could rub off, who knows. Maybe you win an Oscar. Thank us, your acceptance speech. My good friends, colleagues.

LEXINGTON: I told you.

VEGAS: Don't start with me.

LEXINGTON: This is what we get for wantin' to be in show business. Succumbing to the lure.

VEGAS: You know what they say. Apropos show business. Be careful who you get in bed with. You lie down with whores, don't be surprised you get up with clap. Or somethin' worse. Somethin' terminal.

(Pause)

JULIA: What can I do?

LEXINGTON: I wonder what really happened. I see several scenarios. Yours.

VEGAS: Unforeseen offshore snafu. Fire. Money and husband, burned to a fare thee well. Double whammy. What's a grief-stricken widow to do?

JULIA: Yes.

LEXINGTON: Or. The money wasn't in the house.

JULIA: What do you mean?

LEXINGTON: Maybe you took the cash to Cabo with you. Pretty nice nest egg. Screw show business. Spend the rest a your life fuckin' Danny under the coconut palms. Then the fire. The perfect out. Stash the dough in Mexico. Come back, blow smoke up our nose, cry some crocodile tears at the funeral. Perfect. Takes balls.

JULIA: No.

LEXINGTON: Or. Here's an interesting one. Ray took the money.

JULIA: Ray is dead.

LEXINGTON: So you say. Ray took the money. Peeked in the package. Biggest fire a the century. The door swings open. The main chance. Hallelujah. He thinks, fuck the prearrangements. Take the money and run. Sorry, honey. Doesn't mean I don't love you. But let's face it. Seven million dollars is seven million dollars.

VEGAS: Res ipsa loquitor.

LEXINGTON: Fuck's that?

VEGAS: Thing speaks for itself.

LEXINGTON: No shit.

VEGAS: Cheer up, Julia. Maybe he'll drop you a postcard from Belize.

JULIA: They found his body.

VEGAS: They found *a* body. Not even. Bits and pieces. Bits and pieces.

JULIA: I told you. The money was at the house. Ray was to take the money to the banker as soon as everything was in place. I left town. I went to Cabo. To distance myself. To provide deniability.

VEGAS: To get laid.

JULIA: That was lagniappe.

ACT ONE   43

LEXINGTON: Fuck's lagniappe?

JULIA: A little something extra. A little something on the side. As we say in New Orleans.

VEGAS: You from New Orleans?

JULIA: Originally.

VEGAS: Never been to New Orleans.

JULIA: You should go. So. When I got home, everything was fucked up. Ray was dead, the money was gone. End of story.

VEGAS: Not quite.

(Pause)

LEXINGTON: She's cool. Gotta hand it to her. Ice water veins.

VEGAS: Why we got in bed with her. In the first place.

LEXINGTON: I'm gonna call you Ice Water from now on. Instead a partner. We know a few things, too.

JULIA: I'm sure you do.

LEXINGTON: How many things we know?

VEGAS: At least three. Probably more.

LEXINGTON: We know your banker.

JULIA: Oh? Who would that be?

LEXINGTON: Mr. Souza. Chinese-Portuguese guy from Macao. Am I warm, Ice Water?

JULIA: Lukewarm.

LEXINGTON: We had a chat with Mr. Souza. He said he was expecting an initial deposit in the neighborhood a five million dollars.

VEGAS: We said seven.

LEXINGTON: He said five. Said you told him to expect five. He seemed quite certain on this particular point. This was a discrepancy.

VEGAS: A two-million-dollar discrepancy. If I remember the arithmetic the nuns taught me.

LEXINGTON: A nice segue. Brings us to the second thing we know. We know you're in bed with someone else.

VEGAS: Coupla rug merchants of our acquaintance.

JULIA: Rug merchants?

VEGAS: Standard ethnic epithet. Armenians.

LEXINGTON: Ron 'n Tony. Crack 'n smack.

VEGAS: You're a girl got a lotta guys. Popular. Lined up around the block. In bed with so many partners, must get confusing. James. Danny. Me 'n Lex. Mr. Souza. The rug merchants. Anybody else? Hope you use prophylactics.'Cause you're fuckin' a lot of people.

(Pause)

LEXINGTON: How much?

JULIA: Three hundred percent. Guaranteed.

VEGAS: Dream on.

JULIA: They promised me a quick return on my investment. I needed more money for a bankable star. Foreign presale.

LEXINGTON: I mean, how much you invest with our friends Ron 'n Tony?

JULIA: Two million. I held five back. To deposit with Mr. Souza.

VEGAS: Sure.

JULIA: I swear.

LEXINGTON: Don't swear, Ice Water. Tell me somethin'. This windfall profit a three hundred percent. You planning to share that with us? Partner?

JULIA: Fuck, no. I was planning to put it all back in the movie.

LEXINGTON: I like your balls. I have to admire your balls.

VEGAS: Heard from Ron 'n Tony?

JULIA: Not lately.

LEXINGTON: Took a powder, didn't they? So to speak. Tell you what they been up to recently. Blew away some used car dealer.

VEGAS: Dumb fucks.

JULIA: Why?

LEXINGTON: He sold them a lemon. Who knows? Some Armenian thing. Militant bullshit. Used the money you gave 'em to finance their pathetic operation.

JULIA: Fuck.

(Pause)

JULIA: You know where they are.

VEGAS: That's the third thing. Third thing we know. You thinkin' what I'm thinkin'?

LEXINGTON: Recoverable. Part of it, anyway. Still leaves us short five, and change.

VEGAS: Which maybe you stashed in Cabo. Insurance. 'Case the deal with Ron 'n Tony went south. Which it appears to have done in a hurry.

JULIA: Ray is dead. The money was in the house. The five million. It *burned*. Ron and Tony ripped me off for the other two. That's the reality.

LEXINGTON: So you say.

VEGAS: Not one of the things we know. For a fact.

LEXINGTON: What's that word? Lagniappe?

JULIA: Lagniappe.

LEXINGTON: We got a lagniappe for you. Partner.

(Pause)

LEXINGTON: Ever been to Key West?

(She looks back and forth between them, wondering.)

Scene Nine

(Slide: Key West. The Smudgy Cockatiel.)

(Sunset. The veranda of a Victorian gingerbread hotel. Potted palms, flowers, Japanese lanterns. A breeze. A combo plays. A LOUNGE SINGER sings Jamaica Farewell. *He finishes. The very slightest smattering of applause from the few people sitting on the porch, including* RAY, *who is with an attractive woman,* MAX.*)*

LOUNGE SINGER: Thank you. Thank you. I'm gonna take a short break now for sex on the beach.

(Rimshot)

LOUNGE SINGER: That's a drink. With rum. Safe sex on the beach is without the rum.

(Rimshot)

LOUNGE SINGER: Sorta like a Virgin Mary. Shirley Temple. Nancy Reagan. Tipper Gore. Hello? You all come in the same car?

(Rimshot)

LOUNGE SINGER: Like they say, not a dry seat in the house. But seriously. Ladies and germs. We'll be back after a brief pause for some serious altitude adjustment. In the meantime, let's have a big hand for the band. They're Doing The Best They Can. That's the name of the band, not necessarily the opinion of the management. C'mon, give it up. Give it up for They're Doing The Best They Can. Yeah. Alright. Yahoo. Oh, boy.

(He exits into the lobby.)

RAY: They're good. They're really pretty good.
They're not that good.

MAX: *(Southern accent)* Let's have another mai-tai,
they'll get better again.

(She holds up two fingers and signals a WAITRESS.*)*

WAITRESS: Mas mai-tais?

MAX: Por favor. So. Ray—

RAY: Max.

MAX: That's my name. Don't wear it out.

RAY: How'd you ever get a name like Max? I like
women with men's names. Max. Sam. Michael.
Turns me on.

MAX: Whatever floats your boat, sugar. Now, listen.
There's some parts of your story I don't quite
understand.

RAY: Like what?

MAX: Your house burned down.

RAY: Right.

MAX: While your wife was in Cabo San Lucas.

RAY: Right.

MAX: With her boyfriend. The stunt man. Screwin' her
brains out.

RAY: We don't know that.

MAX: We can imagine. Listen, you don't go to a foreign
country to commit adultery and then not commit it,
if you know what I mean.

RAY: You're probably right.

MAX: Okay. She's in Mexico. Screwin' her brains out.
And in general, your domestic situation sucks. Is that
a fair summation?

RAY: Close enough.

MAX: So this fire comes along. The window of opportunity opens and you dive through it, and disappear. Here's my question. Why?

RAY: What do you mean?

MAX: Your wife's actin' like a crazed mink, why not just call a lawyer? Get a divorce.

RAY: That wouldn't've changed anything. Don't you see? Married, divorced, dead. Bing, bing, bing. Same old conveyor belt. Same old station stop on the same old commuter train everyone else is on. Didn't you ever want to start over? Burn off your old life? Make a clean break? Go somewhere you don't know anyone and no one knows you? Where nobody has any assumptions about who you are? That fire. I saw that fire and I felt—blessed. Ecstatic. Free. Everything I owned. Papers. Photos. Family heirlooms. All my personal possessions. Gone. Up in flames. Like shedding an old skin. All that baggage. That history. That old life that didn't work. That I'd fucked up from day one. Melted away. I saw myself floating up from the flames like the phoenix. I could walk away from all that. Spit out the ashes. Reinvent myself.

(Pause)

RAY: So I bugged out. Got on a plane to someplace I'd never been before. Cool my heels and think about how to do this. How to disappear. How to reincarnate.

MAX: Seems extreme. But I understand the impulse. I've been there once or twice myself. Light out for the territory and don't look back. It's very American.

RAY: Huckleberry Finn.

MAX: So you go to Seattle. Somewhere you don't know a living soul. You get lucky, first thing. Find yourself a Cuban-American princess from Tampa who claims her Daddy killed Kennedy. Don't walk away, Renee.

RAY: Pretty weird, I admit.

MAX: Even weirder, a few days later you pick up a copy of the *Chronicle* at an outa town newspaper stand. There's your name, a picture of the grieving widow. They've identified your remains. Found a body. Whose?

RAY: A looter, maybe. Somebody who was in the wrong place at the wrong time. Who knows? Unlucky for him. Lucky for me. Makes me not missing. Makes me dead.

MAX: So now you're deceased. You roll clear across the country to start your new life. Rollin' on the bias to the end of the line. Until you can't roll any further. Like a cue ball rollin' on a downhill slant toward the corner pocket of a table on the tilt. A straight shot. Like you're on a wire. A track. And you drop plop in the pocket here in Key West. With all the rest of us left over, burnt out, semiretired, freelance drug dealers, gun runners, dope smugglers, sponge divers, snook fishermen, con artists, right-wing Cuban terrorists, beatnik hippie homosexuals, assorted social misfits, full-time professional beach combers, conchs, shrimpers, suckers, and spies.

RAY: Don't forget drunks.

MAX: Drunk is redundant in Key West, darlin'.

RAY: Happy to be here.

MAX: Happy you're here. This is the place, baby. The original on the lam, in a jam, made in the shade, don't ask too many questions, place. You know, they used to deliberately set the lights in the channel to lure ships onto the reef. Then they'd go out and salvage the wrecks. Console the survivors. Chuck 'em under the chin. Give 'em some hot coffee, dry drawers, and a ticket on the next train outa town. Wreckin' was *the* major industry. Cigars and shrimp a distant second. By the way. What's your last name? Did you say?

RAY: Which one? My old one, or my new one?

MAX: Either.

(Pause)

MAX: Pretty tall tale, Ray.

RAY: You don't believe me?

MAX: I have my doubts. I admit. A little skeptical around the edges.

RAY: What'd I leave out?

MAX: For starters, you say you want to burn off your old life and disappear down the rabbit hole, but you don't do anything about your appearance. Grow a mustache. Dye your hair. You don't even change your first name. And as soon as you get to town, launch your new life, you take up with some strange woman, tell her the whole crazy scheme.

RAY: I felt I could trust you.

MAX: Jury's still out.

(Pause. RAY smiles.)

RAY: It's a screenplay.

MAX: Thought so. Thought you made it up.

RAY: I wanted to try it out on you. Crack a bottle of champagne over my story, and see if it would make it over the reef to open water. My real name's Ray Avila, not Raymond Gaines. I'm not married. I'm not dead. I don't live in the Bay Area. My house did not burn down.

MAX: Thanks a lot. How'm I 'sposed to trust you now? First thing, before we've even slept together, you tell me a whopper.

RAY: Pretty entertaining, though.

MAX: Mildly entertaining.

RAY: More than mildly.

MAX: Needs work.

RAY: I admit.

MAX: How's it turn out?

RAY: I don't know yet.

MAX: Some story. Got a title?

RAY: *Dark Rapture.* As in, you never know.

MAX: You never know, what?

RAY: You never know what's out there, lurchin' in the dark rapture.

MAX: I'm not familiar with that particular saying.

RAY: Cambodia. Used to say that in Cambodia. Seemed appropriate. You never did know. And the rapture was very dark. Very dark indeed.

(Pause)

RAY: They used helicopters in Southeast Asia. You may have heard. And some of these pilots. Show boats. Liked to clip the tops of the trees. Fly as low as possible over the rice paddies. Churn the surf. The real macho hot shots would bomb down these dirt roads, nothin' more than tracks through the jungle, six or so feet off the ground, strafing everything in sight, blowing up water buffalos, having a great time. So what the VC'd do, Khmer Rouge, Pathet Lao, whatever, they'd string a wire across the road, or a rope, between the trees. First thing in the morning, here comes hot shot, hell bent for leather, whompa whompa whompa, twing. Hits that wire, clips his rotors, goes up in a fire ball. Whoosh. Which event I always thought was the war in a nutshell. All it took to even the playing field, bridge the gap in technology, bring down a multimillion-dollar machine, was a piece of wire strung across the road.

(Pause)

MAX: You were a helicopter pilot?

RAY: Door gunner. Strafing those villes. I was the guy, after interrogation at five hundred feet, used to kick the prisoners out the door.

(Pause)

RAY: Kidding. I'm kidding.

(Pause)

RAY: I was a door gunner on a Huey. But I never kicked anyone into the ether.

(The combo starts in on Margaritaville.*)*

MAX: C'mon. Let's go dance barefoot on the beach.

*(*MAX *pulls* RAY *out of his seat and onto the dance floor.)*

RAY: I lit up an elephant once. A thousand rounds. Dissolved in a big pink cloud.

MAX: Liar. You are some liar. *Ray.*

RAY: I went to college with a pathological liar. A liar of Pinocchio proportions. Certifiable. World-class liar. He'd make up the most outrageous stories. Scary part was, he seemed to believe them. Everything he said. Every last lie. I thought he should be institutionalized. Instead, he grew up to be a presidential speechwriter. He's in Washington working for the current administration, as we speak. It's true, I swear.

*(*MAX *takes* RAY *by the hand and leads him toward the beach. The combo and* LOUNGE SINGER *continue with* Margaritaville. BABCOCK *appears on the veranda. Slow fade to black. End Act One.)*

Act Two

Scene Ten

(Slide: Key West. The Smudgy Cockatiel.)

(Sunset. RAY and MAX are the only customers. The veranda is otherwise deserted. The light is hallucinatory, strange, violet and pearl-colored. A stiff breeze is blowing.)

RAY: God, the light's strange. Looks bruised.

MAX: Hurricane light. All purple and mother-of-pearl.

RAY: I shoulda gone to the Bahamas yesterday, like I planned.

MAX: Ever wonder why, in the movies, they like to have wild, passionate, out of control sex standing up against a wall? Preferably in public?

RAY: Often. Every waking moment.

MAX: I mean, this is completely mythological. Some weird Hollywood idea of a good time. Our eyes meet. We kiss. Suddenly we're chewing each other's lips off. We're knocking furniture over in a mad dash to get to the nearest wall. You slam me, bam, up against the wall, I hike up my skirt, wrap my legs around your waist, rip rip rip, my blouse, your shirt, my panties, your pants, fabric fabric fabric, buttons buttons buttons, pop pop pop, you're magically hard as a rock, I'm miraculously prelubricated, we maneuver everything just so, I slip you in, ooo eee ah, a perfect fit, we have an immediate volcanic simultaneous orgasm without benefit of protracted foreplay, or formal introduction,

all in an impossible, uncomfortable, positively painful
position while you throw your back out, and I scrape
every last inch of skin off my shoulder blades. Which
is exactly what you would expect to result from having
wild, out-of-control, wake the entire neighborhood,
bump-and-grind, howl at the moon sex, up against
a stucco wall. I mean, why don't they just lie down?
Get horizontal like the rest of us.

RAY: I don't know. Looks better for the camera.

MAX: I guess. But, you ever try that for real? Doesn't
work. Angles are all wrong. I mean, where's the
attraction? You always end up on the floor anyway.
Gravity dictates.

RAY: What do you think? I guess it's too late to leave
town. Maybe we should have.

MAX: Poor Ray. You were just passing through, weren't
you? Then you met me.

RAY: Yeah. Blew my itinerary.

MAX: We'll just hang tight. Weather the storm.
I like hurricanes. We'll be okay. Where's the waitress?
I want another mai-tai.

RAY: Battening down the hotel hatches. Hurricane
shutters. Hurricane lamps.

MAX: We'll get drunk and watch the palm trees bend
over parallel to the ground. Always exciting.

RAY: This is my first hurricane.

MAX: They're fun. Scary as shit.

RAY: At this point, I don't think we have any choice.

(Pause)

MAX: Ray. You know, I was looking for. Well. I was
basically going through your drawers. Snooping
around. I wanted to read your script. I didn't find it.

RAY: Script's not in my drawers.

MAX: I found some other stuff. Passport. With your picture. Some other stuff says you're you. Sorry. I like you. I'm a suspicious bitch. I wanted to make sure. I mean, you are some liar. We know that's true.

RAY: Should I ask you for your ID?

MAX: I'd be hard pressed to prove everything I've told you. I tend to exaggerate a little. Embroider around the edges. Most of it's more or less factual. I found the clipping. About the fire. How they found this fella's body. Gaines? About his wife. A picture of the grieving widow.

(Pause)

RAY: Research. Where I got the idea.

MAX: I thought you made that story up.

RAY: I did. Most of it. Clipping was just a point of departure.

MAX: I apologize for going through your things.

RAY: Don't worry about it. Script's in the closet. I'll dig it out. If you really wanna read it.

MAX: In the suitcases?

RAY: You go through those, too?

MAX: Course not. They were locked. I didn't have the moxie to try and jimmy 'em.

RAY: Nothin' in 'em but scripts. Papers. Contracts. Bullshit. My life is about little scraps of paper.

MAX: Efficiency experts say you should only handle a piece of paper no more than one time. It's in your hand, then it's outa your life.

RAY: Interesting.

MAX: Before I was a drug dealer, I was an efficiency expert. And before I was an efficiency expert, I was an exotic dancer. Princess Totempole. I had a black wig,

and a pair of trained ravens, who would pluck the
scarves off my body, one by one.

RAY: Trained ravens.

MAX: Tristan and Isolde. They were very talented. And
then when Tristan and Isolde got too old to pluck, I put
out to pasture the black wig and started performing
under the stage name of Miss Cherry Bounce.

RAY: Miss Cherry Bounce.

MAX: After the drink. Cherry bounce.

RAY: I'm not familiar with that particular drink.

MAX: It's a southern concoction. Cherries marinated
in vodka and pure grain alcohol. Packs a wallop.
The highlight of my act as Miss Cherry Bounce was
an interpretive dance to the theme from *Perry Mason*.

(She scats some bars, mimes a few moves. Sexy and very
dramatic.)

MAX: It was wildly popular.

RAY: I'll bet.

*(*BABCOCK *strolls onto the veranda, sits at the next table.)*

BABCOCK: Hey.

MAX: Hello.

BABCOCK: I know you.

RAY: I don't think so. Sorry. Can't think where.

BABCOCK: Ever spend time in the Bay Area?

RAY: Not to speak of.

BABCOCK: Well. Who knows? It'll come to me.
Mind if I join you?

MAX: Hey. Lifeboat party. More the merrier.

*(*BABCOCK *pulls up a chair at their table.)*

BABCOCK: I'm Babcock.

RAY: Ray Avila. And this is Max.

BABCOCK: Max. Pleased to meet you.

MAX: Ditto, I'm sure.

BABCOCK: Max. What is that short for? Maxine?

MAX: Margaret.

BABCOCK: Margaret. Really. I like that.

(BABCOCK *looks around for the* WAITRESS.)

BABCOCK: Kinda slow. Who do you have to know to get a drink in this stellar establishment?

MAX: They're all inside, getting ready for Hurricane Lazlo.

BABCOCK: Lazlo? This is a Hungarian hurricane?

RAY: I'll go to the bar. What do you want?

MAX: Mai-tai.

BABCOCK: Cuba libre.

RAY: Right back.

(RAY *exits into the hotel.*)

BABCOCK: Remember when hurricanes had women's names? I'm nostalgic for that era. Hurricane Annabella. First hurricane of the season. Never been in a hurricane myself. Bound to happen.

MAX: How so?

BABCOCK: Cataclysmic natural disasters just seem to follow me around. Been in earthquakes, bad ones. Eruptions. Floods. Tidal waves. Typhoons. Blizzards. Big big fires. Read about the recent Bay Area blaze?

MAX: Yeah. As a matter of fact.

BABCOCK: I witnessed that up close. Chaos. Sheer chaos.

MAX: Really. You live there?

BABCOCK: No. Lucky for me. Just visiting. I know Ray from somewhere. Tell me. You know, was he ever in the service? Southeast Asia?

MAX: Not that I know of.

BABCOCK: I thought maybe. Cambodia. Probably not. Long time ago. So. Max. What it is you do?

MAX: A little of this, a little of that. Like everyone in Key West. In the summer we live off the fish. In the winter we live off the Yankees.

BABCOCK: I know what you mean. A little of this, a little of that. Me, too.

(Pause. They trade smiles.)

BABCOCK: What line a work is Ray in?

MAX: Screenwriter.

BABCOCK: Really. How unusual. Must be exciting.

MAX: You don't sound like a Yankee.

BABCOCK: What do I sound like?

MAX: I don't know. Can't quite place it.

BABCOCK: Maybe I'll go see can I help Ray with the drinks. Back in a flash.

MAX: 'Kay.

(BABCOCK exits into the hotel. The light darkens. The wind comes up. The rain starts.)

Scene Eleven

(Slide: Key West. The Smudgy Cockatiel.)

(Morning. The veranda. BABCOCK is smoking a cigarette. LEXINGTON, VEGAS, and JULIA come out of the hotel.)

VEGAS: Which way's Cuba?

BABCOCK: That way.

VEGAS: See it from here?

BABCOCK: Ninety miles. Look at that surf. Killer surf.

VEGAS: What was it like?

BABCOCK: Exciting. No other word for it.

VEGAS: Sorry we missed it. Stuck in Miami. They closed the airport. I never been in a hurricane. One a my unfulfilled aspirations. This place held up pretty good.

BABCOCK: Hey. These old buildings. They knew whereof. Built for the weather. You know? Not like this new condo shit. Windows fall out when somebody slams the door. Plus. We were lucky. A mile from here there's nothin' standing. Looks like Hirofuckingshima. Palm fronds all over the place.

LEXINGTON: You through?

(Pause)

BABCOCK: Don't know how he coulda got off the island.

LEXINGTON: By boat. Would be my guess. This being an island and all.

BABCOCK: Maybe he had time to get up to the next Key before the hurricane hit. Be foolish to try.

VEGAS: Plus, the desk clerk. Said he had a coupla heavy suitcases. Which are nowhere to be found.

LEXINGTON: Ray comes outa the men's room. Spots Babcock in the bar, talking to this Max girl. He runs upstairs. Grabs his suitcases. Down the back stairs. Runs down to the dock. Persuades some Bahamian fisherman take him up the next Key. With a hurricane comin'? You buy that?

VEGAS: Maybe he didn't grab the suitcases. Maybe she did. The girlfriend.

LEXINGTON: Max.

VEGAS: Ray sees Babcock, figures the jig is up. Goes out the rear exit. Clothes on his back. Gives him a fighting chance. While Babcock is out lookin' for him in the middle of Hurricane fuckin' Lazlo, Max grabs the bags. Buries 'em in her back yard.

LEXINGTON: Permutations. Fuckin' permutations are drivin' me batshit.

BABCOCK: I'll go toss her place.

LEXINGTON: Not yet.

JULIA: Wasn't Ray.

LEXINGTON: Then who? Wasn't Ray, then who?

JULIA: Ray is dead.

LEXINGTON: Goin' by the name of Ray Avila.

JULIA: If it is Ray, and he did take the money, why would he call himself Ray Avila? Avila's a Spanish name.

BABCOCK: Cuban, actually.

VEGAS: Life's little mysteries.

BABCOCK: She told me he was a screenwriter.

JULIA: Who isn't?

LEXINGTON: Wasn't your husband, then who?

VEGAS: Fits the description.

LEXINGTON: We describe him, everybody says, yeah, sounds like the guy. What more do you want? What else do we have to go on? In the absence of a fuckin' photograph.

(JULIA *gives him a look.*)

LEXINGTON: I know, I know. Don't tell me. The fire.

VEGAS: Awful convenient.

JULIA: Ray was average. When you describe Ray, you describe a lot of guys.

VEGAS: If Babcock had seen him, we'd know.

LEXINGTON: Yeah. We'd know was it the same guy he talked to the night of the fire.

BABCOCK: Missed him by that much. Hey. Know what I think? I think this guy, whoever he is, Ray Avila, Ray Gaines, just ran outa luck. If the fire didn't get him, the hurricane did. The snook are feedin' on him as we speak.

LEXINGTON: Babcock. Ever been to Tampa?

BABCOCK: Sure. Alla time. Excellent Cuban food.

LEXINGTON: Bring me back a plate a ropa vieja.

(BABCOCK *puts out his cigarette, exits into the hotel.* JULIA *looks at* LEXINGTON.)

JULIA: What's in Tampa?

LEXINGTON: Busch Gardens.

(Pause)

JULIA: What now? May I ask?

LEXINGTON: We'll hang out. Eat some conch fritters. Go talk to Miss Max. See if she has any fresh dug holes in her back yard. It'll be fun. Treasure hunt. Then we'll go down the end of Duvall Street. Watch the sunset. Look for the famous flash a green.

VEGAS: Get Jimmy Buffet's autograph.

LEXINGTON: Tomorrow we'll go back to Miami. Drop a dime on our friends in the rug racket.

(He looks at JULIA.)

LEXINGTON: Okay with you? Partner?

JULIA: You weren't gonna call me that.

(The WAITRESS *comes out onto the veranda.)*

WAITRESS: What'll it be?

VEGAS: Mai-tais all around.

WAITRESS: You got it.

(She exits into the hotel. VEGAS *looks at* JULIA.)

VEGAS: Are we having fun yet? Julia?

(JULIA *looks at him, gets up, goes into the hotel.*)

VEGAS: What's in Tampa?

LEXINGTON: Calls to Ray Avila from a pay phone in Ybor City to here at the Smudgy Cockatiel on a regular basis. Desk clerk said it was always the same woman.

VEGAS: Not much to go on.

LEXINGTON: How'd he get off the island? Guy's good.

VEGAS: Not that good. Maybe Babcock's right. Maybe he didn't. Maybe he's fish food.

LEXINGTON: Fuckin' Babcock. Had him between his thumb and forefinger.

VEGAS: Yeah. We have to do something about that.

(Pause)

VEGAS: Missed him by that much. You buy that?

LEXINGTON: No.

VEGAS: Me either.

LEXINGTON: Said he got a tip.

VEGAS: Yeah. But instead a meeting us in Miami as per our instructions, he goes on ahead, gets here first, spooks him.

LEXINGTON: Fuckin' Babcock. What's he up to?

VEGAS: He's got the hook in. Deep. Playin' this Avila guy like a bone fish, givin' him lotsa line, lettin' him run, hopin' he'll run to the money. Babcock won't reel him in 'til he's sure, one way or the other. Is this guy really Ray Gaines, where's the money.

LEXINGTON: Babcock, Babcock, Babcock. Scammin' us all the way. Problem is, so much loose cash floatin' around, nobody's inclined to share.

VEGAS: Isn't that always the problem, these situations? Chum's in the water.

LEXINGTON: Fuck's chum?

VEGAS: You know. Blood. Guts. Gets 'em excited.

LEXINGTON: Feeding frenzy.

VEGAS: Exactly.

(LEXINGTON *stands.*)

LEXINGTON: Let's go talk to Miss Max.

VEGAS: What about the mai-tais?

LEXINGTON: Fuck the mai-tais.

(LEXINGTON *exits into the hotel, passing the* WAITRESS *on her way out with a tray of four mai-tais.*)

WAITRESS: Where'd everybody go?

VEGAS: Somethin' came up.

(*He lays a fifty on her tray.*)

VEGAS: Put those in a go cup for me, will ya, darlin'?

WAITRESS: No problem.

(*She follows him in.*)

Scene Twelve

(*Slide: Tampa*)

(*Night. A half-darkened kitchen.* BABCOCK *is sitting at a Formica table in his undershirt, eating yucca and drinking beer. He's sweating, mopping his brow with a paper towel. He hears the front door lock turn, and stops eating. Listens intently. Footsteps move through the next room and stop just outside.*)

BABCOCK: Renee? Mi hija?

(*Pause.* RON *and* TONY *come into the kitchen.*)

BABCOCK: Oh, boy.

TONY: What smells?

BABCOCK: Garlic and lemon.

TONY: What're you eating? Garlic soup?

BABCOCK: Yucca.

TONY: Fuck's yucca?

BABCOCK: It's good. It's a tuber. Want some?

TONY: No, thanks.

BABCOCK: Lexington and Vegas are looking for you.

TONY: They found us.

RON: Why we're here.

TONY: Help you out.

BABCOCK: How so?

TONY: We cut a deal. This your house?

BABCOCK: No.

TONY: You look pretty much to home.

BABCOCK: I know the person owns this place. I stay here when I'm in town.

RON: Renee?

BABCOCK: Yeah. What kinda deal?

TONY: Lexington and Vegas. Had we known.

RON: Never. We're not crazy.

TONY: We figured this Hollywood producer. This Julia Gaines girl. Song and dance about Hong Kong investors. She wants to get into wholesale product. Okay. Rip her off. Who's she gonna tell?

RON: Her agent?

TONY: She gonna tell her agent a coupla dealers ripped me off, do somethin' about it? I don't think so.

RON: Turns out these Hong Kong investors turn out to be Lexington and Vegas. Oh, shit.

TONY: Holy shit. Luckily, she backs us up on this.

BABCOCK: Julia.

TONY: Right. That we had no idea. In the dark.
We came this close. Lexington and Vegas are not
guys to fuck around with. I like your house.

BABCOCK: I told you. Not mine.

TONY: Still. Nice.

RON: Also luckily, we still had most of the dough.

TONY: Kills me. But. What can you do? Who's Renee?

BABCOCK: My daughter.

TONY: She around?

BABCOCK: No. She's outa town. Why I'm staying here.

TONY: But when we came in. You thought it might be
her.

BABCOCK: I didn't know. Who else had a key?

TONY: Us, actually.

BABCOCK: So you pay the money back. Most of it.

TONY: Yeah. Kills me. We had a sweet sweet deal lined
up.

RON: Arms for Armenia.

BABCOCK: Catchy.

TONY: First-class ordnance. State of the art
antipersonnel devices.

RON: A little something for the old country.

TONY: These Azerbaijani fucks. Turks by another name.
And, let's face it. A Christian island in a Muslim sea.
All those people are Turks. One kind or another. So the
kin folk could use some help. But. What can you do?

RON: We'll promote something else.

TONY: We paid back what we had. Said they'd forgive
the rest. Clear our tab. On condition we pitch in.

BABCOCK: Help me find Ray.

TONY: General idea.

RON: Got any hunches?

BABCOCK: What'd they turn up at the girlfriend's?

TONY: Max?

BABCOCK: I take it not the money.

TONY: Not the money nor Ray nor this Max girl neither. She was outa there so fast she forgot to turn her Mr. Coffee off. Melted the element.

RON: Any idea where we should look next?

BABCOCK: I think maybe he went to New Orleans.

TONY: The Crescent City.

RON: What makes you think that?

BABCOCK: Maybe you should check it out.

RON: Maybe we will.

TONY: Why don't you tag along?

BABCOCK: I'll join you there. Leave word. Gotta touch base with Lexington and Vegas.

TONY: Let's go now. Their idea.

BABCOCK: Mind if I call 'em?

RON: Feel free.

(Pause)

BABCOCK: Now?

TONY: Why not?

BABCOCK: Middle of the fuckin' night for Christ's sake. Next plane's tomorrow morning.

TONY: We'll drive.

BABCOCK: You serious?

RON: It'll be fun. Watchin' the sun come up on The Redneck Riviera. Beautiful.

TONY: C'mon. Throw some stuff in a bag. Let's go.

BABCOCK: Okay. Sure.

(BABCOCK *pushes back from the table. As he gets up he picks up his plate of yucca and his beer bottle and takes a step towards the sink. Moving suddenly, he hurls his plate in* RON's *face and breaks the bottle across* TONY's. *He tries for the door.* TONY *tackles him, puts a gun to his head, and a knee in his back.*)

TONY: Stop. Stop now. Just stop. I don't wanna have to whack you in your daughter's house.

(BABCOCK *lies still.*)

RON: You okay? Got blood all over.

TONY: You can drive me to the emergency room later. Sew my fucking ear back on. Toss the rest of the house.

(RON *exits.* TONY *stands.*)

TONY: Stay down. Don't do anything stupid.

(*He finds a cloth, holds it to the side of his head.*)

TONY: Babcock. What kind a name is Babcock?

BABCOCK: I don't know.

TONY: When'd you change it?

BABCOCK: I never changed it. Not like some.

TONY: So what is Babcock? Alias?

BABCOCK: Nom de guerre.

TONY: Fuck's that mean? Who are you when you're at home?

BABCOCK: Chibas. Jose Marti Chibas Valenzuela.

TONY: That's a mouthful. A Cubano mouthful.

BABCOCK: Chinga tu madre.

TONY: Now, I know what that means.

(RON *enters the room, carrying something wrapped in soft black cloth. He puts it on the table.*)

RON: Look at this.

(TONY *unwraps the bundle. Inside is a high-powered sharpshooting rifle, in pieces, immaculately kept. He holds it up to the light.*)

TONY: Well well well. What do you hunt, Chibas? Deer?

BABCOCK: Javalinas.

RON: Fuck's a javalina?

BABCOCK: Wild pigs.

(TONY *examines the rifle.*)

TONY: A real collector's item. Circa 1960. Cherry. You don't use this much.

BABCOCK: Once or twice.

TONY: A real museum piece.

(*Pause. He looks at* RON.)

TONY: Put it back. Leave her something to remember her Daddy by.

(RON *shrugs. Wraps up the rifle, exits.*)

TONY: Go ahead. Get up.

(BABCOCK *gets up.*)

TONY: Let's go for a drive.

BABCOCK: New Orleans?

TONY: See how far we get.

(BABCOCK *exits.* TONY *follows him. As he leaves the room, he turns off the kitchen light, leaving it in darkness.*)

Scene Thirteen

(*Slide: New Orleans. The Napoleon House.*)

(*Afternoon.* RAY *and* RENEE *are sitting at a table, drinking Pimm's Cups. The door is open to the sidewalk. Light and air are streaming in.*)

RAY: Everywhere I go has peaked. Hawaii. Key West. Greenwich Village. Puerto Vallarta. Katmandu. You should have seen it back when. Before it got popular. Before the tourists slash criminals slash developers ruined it. It was something in the old days. Boy. Things ain't what they used to be. Too bad. Shoulda seen it. Shoulda been there. Mexico. Tahiti. Bali. Big Sur. Whole fuckin' world's past its prime. But. But I like it here. You do? You like this? This is nothing. Shoulda seen it before it got ruined. Before it got fucked up. Say that about New Orleans, too. Crime. Kids on bicycles with automatic weapons. Can't go out after dark. Too many tourists. Too much graft. You should been here back in the days it really was The City That Care Forgot. By which I suspect a lotta people mean, before black folks got the vote. The Planet of New Orleans. Been in decline since the Civil War. So to say New Orleans is past its prime is really beside the point.

RENEE: Your wife was from New Orleans?

RAY: Originally.

RENEE: You're divorced?

RAY: She's deceased.

RENEE: Sorry.

RAY: Yeah. I like it here. I like you can sit on the east bank of the Mississippi, and watch the sun come up over the West Bank. Place is surreal. I like the decay. I like the humidity. I like the way the sewers back up when it rains. I like the above-ground cemeteries, the dripping walls, the hurricanes, the whole below sea-level soggy underfoot suck your sneakers off swamp thang program. Everything damp. Decadent. Rotten. Basically I like New Orleans because it looks and smells and tastes like a tropical cathouse.

RENEE: I have something to tell you.

RAY: You're married.

RENEE: No.

RAY: You're gay.

RENEE: I don't think so. I lied to you. About my father. About Popi.

RAY: He didn't kill Kennedy.

RENEE: No. I mean, as far as I know, he did.

RAY: That's a relief. I was just glueing my belief system back together. My world view.

RENEE: He's not dead. My dad. I lied about that. But I swore on my mother's memory I'd never tell. And I felt bad about breaking my word. But I had to tell someone. What I told you. About Popi. After all these years. And I felt I could trust you.

RAY: People feel that way. I don't know why.

(Pause)

RENEE: What're we gonna do here?

RAY: Go to Mother's. Get a shrimp po'boy. Drive out St. Claude Avenue to the lower Ninth Ward, take a look at Fats Domino's house. Take a nap. Ruin our livers. All kinds of excitement.

RENEE: That sounds good. Especially the part about the nap.

RAY: Renee. Thanks for meeting me here. Bringing my things.

RENEE: No problem. C'mon, let's go. I'm starving.

(She picks up her purse and strolls out. He downs his drink, and follows.)

Scene Fourteen

(Slide: New Orleans. A hotel room.)

(Night. RAY *is sitting on the bed, his shoes off.* LEXINGTON *is smoking a cigarette.* VEGAS *is scrutinizing* RAY's *passport.)*

LEXINGTON: Well?

*(*VEGAS *shakes his head.)*

VEGAS: Good. Professional. Expensive. Kosher? I don't think so.

(He tosses it to RAY.*)*

VEGAS: How much you pay for it?

LEXINGTON: Who are you?

RAY: That's me.

VEGAS: That's your picture. But your passport's forged. How come you have a forged passport, pal?

RAY: That's my passport.

LEXINGTON: What's your real name?

RAY: It's right there.

LEXINGTON: Ray Avila? I don't think so. I think you're Raymond Gaines. Married to Julia Gaines.

RAY: I'm divorced.

LEXINGTON: I'm not surprised. You being deceased and all. Hell on the home life.

VEGAS: Where's the money?

RAY: I don't have any money. Wish I did.

VEGAS: Let's say you're Ray Gaines. Not Ray Avila. Let's say Ray Avila doesn't exist. Let's say you stole our money. Which we want back.

RAY: No. Sorry.

LEXINGTON: Five million.

RAY: Wouldn't that be nice?

VEGAS: Your wife's parcel. You were supposed to take to Mr. Souza?

RAY: Sorry. Name's Avila. These other people. Ray and Julia Gaines. Souza. I don't know them.

LEXINGTON: Where are the suitcases?

RAY: Suitcases.

VEGAS: You check into a hotel, you got suitcases. Where are they?

RAY: You got the wrong guy.

VEGAS: I don't think so. I think you're Ray Gaines alright. Why didn't you change your first name, Ray, while you were at it?

RAY: I give up. Too much trouble?

VEGAS: No. No, this is trouble. What you got now.

LEXINGTON: If he is Gaines, whose body did they find in the rubble?

VEGAS: The meter reader, who knows? Life's little mysteries.

(The key turns in the lock.)

LEXINGTON: One a which we're about to clear up.

(The door opens. RENEE *enters, carrying a large white paper sack. Starts when she sees* LEXINGTON *and* VEGAS.*)*

LEXINGTON: Who the fuck're you?

RENEE: Who're you?

RAY: This is my friend, Renee.

VEGAS: What's in the bag, Renee?

RENEE: Muffulettas. Want one?

VEGAS: Fuck's a muffuletta?

RENEE: Sandwich. Olive spread and cold cuts.

VEGAS: Sounds horrible.

RENEE: Suit yourself.

(She sits on the bed next to RAY, unwraps the sandwiches, gives one to RAY.)

RAY: You mind?

VEGAS: Be my guest. I personally would not choose something called a muffuletta for my last meal.

RENEE: What does he mean by that? Ray?

RAY: A joke. Relieve the tension.

RENEE: I wasn't tense.

VEGAS: We are.

RENEE: Ray, who are these payasos? They're scaring me.

RAY: They think I'm somebody else. They think I have something of theirs I don't have.

RENEE: What?

LEXINGTON: Five million dollars. Less incidental expenses. Incurred galavanting all over the country.

RENEE: No way. No way he has five million dollars.

VEGAS: How would you know? Renee.

RENEE: I don't. I don't know.

VEGAS: I hope you don't.

(A key turns in the lock.)

VEGAS: That must be the goombahs now.

LEXINGTON: About time.

(The door opens, RON and TONY enter. TONY is carrying two heavy suitcases.)

RON: Look what we found.

(TONY sets the suitcases down.)

TONY: We persuaded the manager to open the office vault.

RON: He didn't wanna do it, but we appealed to his pain threshold.

LEXINGTON: Where's Julia?

RON: In the hall.

LEXINGTON: Ask her to come in.

(RON *opens the door, steps into the hall. Everybody waits. In a moment,* JULIA *steps into the room. She sees* RAY, *stares.* RON *comes in behind her, closes the door. Everybody waits.)*

LEXINGTON: I believe you two. May have met.

JULIA: No.

(Pause)

JULIA: No. Never.

RAY: Mrs. Gaines. I take it.

JULIA: This is not my husband. This is not my Ray. Ray Gaines. Not at all.

VEGAS: You sure?

JULIA: Don't be stupid.

LEXINGTON: Who the fuck are you?

RAY: Avila. Ray Avila.

TONY: Avila. What kinda name is Avila? Spanish?

RAY: Czech, actually.

TONY: Sounds Spanish to me. Cuban.

RON: You got Cubans on the brain.

LEXINGTON: Ice Water. What're you saying?

JULIA: I'm saying I don't know who this man is. I've never seen him before. My husband is dead. He died in the fire. I wish you'd quit torturing me.

(LEXINGTON *turns to* TONY.)

LEXINGTON: What're you waiting for? A papal dispensation? Open 'em.

TONY: Alright. Alright. Don't get your boxers in a wad.

(TONY *picks the locks on the first suitcase.* RON *picks the locks on the second suitcase.* TONY *pops the locks on his suitcase.*)

TONY: Voila.

(*The suitcase is full of scripts.*)

TONY: What the fuck?

RAY: Spec scripts.

(*Pause.* JULIA *starts to laugh, hysterically.*)

JULIA: Spec scripts. Jesus. That's hilarious. Spec scripts. Hee hee. Spec scripts. Whoo. Whoo. Hysterical. You caught yourself a screenwriter. A felonious screenwriter. Congratulations.

(JULIA's *laughter subsides. She stops laughing, wipes tears from her eyes. Looks at* LEXINGTON *and* VEGAS, *who aren't laughing.*)

JULIA: I'm sorry. Inside joke. Spec scripts. Hoo hoo.

(RON *pops the locks on the second suitcase. He turns it over, scattering the contents. It's full of papers.*)

LEXINGTON: Maybe we shoulda held onto Babcock. ID this bird.

TONY: Shoulda thought a that before we went to Tampa.

(LEXINGTON *looks at* RON *and* TONY.)

LEXINGTON: Go on. Get the fuck outa Dodge. We're square.

TONY: Can I get it in writing?

VEGAS: Hey. Up to this moment, contrary to all expectation, you been a coupla very lucky white boys. Don't fuck up your undeserved good fortune.

TONY: You say so. See you around.

RON: Ciao.

(They leave. LEXINGTON *fixes on* RAY. *He draws a gun, points it first at* RAY, *then holds it to* JULIA*'s temple.)*

LEXINGTON: Lie to me, Ice Water. Tell me he's not your husband.

JULIA: No. This man is not my husband.

*(*LEXINGTON *cocks the gun. Points it at* RAY.*)*

LEXINGTON: You don't care? You don't care if I waste this asshole?

JULIA: Be my guest. For all I know, he stole the money. Murdered Ray. Left his body to burn. In fact, do him. Go ahead. Do him. I want you to. Just in case.

(Pause. LEXINGTON *considers.* VEGAS *touches his arm.)*

VEGAS: Lex. Give it up. The money's gone. It's history. It's in the video stores.

(Pause. LEXINGTON *wavers.)*

VEGAS: What'll we do with these loose ends? We can't do 'em here.

(Pause. LEXINGTON *looks them over.)*

JULIA: Who're you talking about?

LEXINGTON: All a you. All three a you.

JULIA: Please.

LEXINGTON: Don't beg, Ice Water. Ruin my image.

(Pause)

JULIA: I think we should resurrect our original arrangement.

(Pause. LEXINGTON *lowers the gun.)*

LEXINGTON: You're kidding.

JULIA: You got most of the two million back from Ron and Tony. I told you I'd pay back the rest.

(Pause)

VEGAS: Whaddya think? Wanna get back in bed with her?

LEXINGTON: She's got balls.

VEGAS: Why we got in bed with her in the first place. Honest mistake. Over ambitious. Took a gamble. Didn't pan out. Wasn't a bad deal. We still need a reliable fluff 'n fold on a regular basis.

JULIA: I'll throw in the money from Ray's life insurance policy. As a token of good faith.

VEGAS: How much you get from that deal?

JULIA: Five hundred K.

VEGAS: That all? You got burned, babe. So? Whaddya think?

LEXINGTON: I don't know. Ice Water. Still got a burning desire to make movies?

JULIA: Of course.

LEXINGTON: We participate from dollar one a the gross.

JULIA: I basically have no problem with that.

LEXINGTON: First, you pay us back the seven million you owe us.

JULIA: Five. You got two back already.

LEXINGTON: Seven. The original five plus two for vigorish and sheer fuckin' aggravation.

JULIA: What choice do I have?

LEXINGTON: None.

JULIA: Sounds wonderful to me.

(Pause)

JULIA: I keep the life insurance money.

LEXINGTON: They just get bigger 'n bigger, don't they? What do you do, sprinkle testosterone on your Lucky Charms?

JULIA: I need to buy a house.

VEGAS: Five hundred K in L.A.? That's a teardown, babe. A fixer-upper in the Valley. You can't buy anything for five hundred K in L.A.—

LEXINGTON: Hey. Hey. Hey. You through? Wait downstairs. Partner.

(JULIA *leaves.*)

VEGAS: So whaddya think?

LEXINGTON: I still think she took the five million in the first place, stashed it in a coconut in Cabo. What the hell. We get some proof? We can always do her later.

VEGAS: See how her first picture turns out. Whack her for sheer aesthetic reasons.

LEXINGTON: Good idea. Furthermore, I feel I should do these two on general principles. Leading us on a wild fucking coast-to-coast goose chase.

VEGAS: Lex—

LEXINGTON: Why do you have a forged passport, pal?

VEGAS: Lex. Lotsa people got forged passports. Including us. Come on. Let's go talk to our new partner. I got an idea I wanna pitch her. For a western. Come on. Let it go. These people are *tourists.*

LEXINGTON: Okay, okay. Fuck. Can't do you here, anyway. Let's get outa here. Fuck.

(*They leave. Pause.* RENEE *looks at* RAY.)

RENEE: Who are you?

RAY: Raymond Avila.

RENEE: Did you take their money?

RAY: No.

RENEE: Who was that woman?

RAY: I don't know. Never saw her before.

RENEE: Then what was that all about?

RAY: Mistake. They mistook me. They thought I was somebody else.

RENEE: Some mistake. That man was talking about killing us. We came this close to being murdered.

RAY: I know. I know.

(Pause)

RAY: Renee. You didn't tell anyone you were meeting me here, did you?

RENEE: No.

(Pause)

RENEE: Just my dad.

(Pause)

RENEE: He wouldn't tell anyone. I trust him.

RAY: You trusted me, too. Shows you what a judge of character you are.

(Pause)

RENEE: Who would he tell? He doesn't have anything to do with these people. These gangsters.

(Pause)

RAY: How did you happen to pick Seattle for a vacation? Did you say?

RENEE: Far away from Tampa as I could get.

(Pause)

RENEE: As much as I like you, Ray, I don't wanna be here if they change their minds and come back.

RAY: Neither do I.

RENEE: I think I better go home now. Call Popi.

(She gets up, goes into the bathroom. RAY takes a bite of his muffuletta.)

Scene Fifteen

(Slide: Los Angeles)

(DANNY's apartment. He is shirtless, lounging on the floor watching a video, eating popcorn. Doorbell rings. He gets up, goes to the door, opens it. JULIA steps in.)

DANNY: Hey.

JULIA: Hey, yourself.

(He gives her a kiss.)

DANNY: Glad to see you. Sight for sore eyes. Come in. You look beat.

JULIA: Rough trip.

(She comes in, sets her bag down.)

DANNY: Make your deal?

JULIA: Yeah. Yeah, I did. I think so. I think it's all coming together. At last.

DANNY: That calls for a celebration. Lemme pop a bottle of Dom.

(He goes in the other room. JULIA collapses for a moment. DANNY returns with a bottle of Dom Perignon and glasses.)

DANNY: You okay?

JULIA: Just jet-lagged. I'll be alright in a minute.

DANNY: So, tell me about your trip. How was New York?

JULIA: Oh, you know. New York.

(He pops the cork.)

DANNY: Yeah. Goin' to hell in a handbasket. New York, New York. Sound so nice, they had to name it twice. Tell me what street compares to Mott Street in July. I'll tell you what street compares to Mott Street in July. Last time I was in New York they were havin' a garbage strike in the middle of the summer. Mott Street was pretty fuckin' ripe. Incomparable. I haven't been back since. What a place. The city so cold it wouldn't give God a break.

(He fills the glasses, hands her one.)

DANNY: Here's to your deal.

JULIA: Yeah. Thanks.

(They clink glasses. Drink.)

DANNY: This is what you wanted. The show business.

JULIA: Lucky me. I'm so lucky. We're all so lucky. Just a lot of lucky so-and-so's.

DANNY: Yeah. I guess we are. Comparatively.

(She drains her glass, puts it down.)

JULIA: Still want to pull my focus?

DANNY: Sure. All night long.

JULIA: Let's go, cowboy. I'm in a mood.

(She walks off. DANNY finishes his drink, picks up the bottle, and follows.)

Scene Sixteen

(Slide: Becquia, St. Vincent. The Frangipani Hotel.)

(Afternoon. The patio. Lots of breeze and tropical light. RAY is lounging in a robe and sandals, talking to someone in the pool.)

RAY: What do you wanna do? We could take the boat over to St. Vincent this afternoon. Walk around

Kingstown. Go up to Round Hill. Look at the view.
Buy fresh bread from the prisoners. Speaking of bread,
we could go to the botanical gardens. Oldest botanical
gardens in the Western Hemisphere. They have the
original breadfruit tree there. The one Captain Bligh
brought from Tahiti to the New World to feed the
slaves. The original Captain Bligh. No kidding. Not the
original breadfruit tree. The original breadfruit tree's
daughter.

(MAX *comes on, out of the pool, wrapping a robe around her.*)

MAX: Whatever you want.

(*She gives him a kiss. Sits next to him.*)

MAX: All this high life. I'm getting too old for it.

RAY: I love this place. The Frangipani. The flamboyant
trees. The star apples. Up on Mt. Pleasant, all those
inbred white people eating mangos. Descendants of
buccaneers. And over on the other side of the island,
the mulatto whalers. Harpoons and open boats. I mean,
there's this whole color caste thing on this tiny island.
Five thousand people. Fascinating. I was talking to the
Prime Minister in the bar last night at jump up.

MAX: His family owns the Frangipani.

RAY: I know. Still. To be chatting with the Prime
Minister of St. Vincent over a couple of cuba libres.
You know he takes the boat back and forth to St.
Vincent everyday? Talks to Parliament. Comes back to
Becquia in the evening, hangs out at the bar. Now that's
my idea of a country. A hundred thousand people. Size
a country should be. We could sail down to Petit St.
Vincent tomorrow.

MAX: Sure. Why not?

RAY: Stay there a coupla days. Sail down to Mustique.
Spend the winter in Grenada.

MAX: Why not? We got time. We're retired. We're rich.

(They kiss.)

MAX: We're so lucky, aren't we?

RAY: We are. Lucky.

(Pause)

RAY: You could've gone anywhere. The window was wide open.

MAX: I thought about it. After you left, and that guy went to look for you and never came back, there I was, sitting on the veranda of the Smudgy Cockatiel, all by myself, drinking a mai-tai, hurricane comin', thinking, oh boy oh boy, is this strange. I went upstairs, got your suitcases, took them to my sister's on the other side of the island. Waited there a few days. Snuck back to my house, which they'd totally trashed. They even dug up the yard. At that point, I didn't know what to do.

RAY: Did you ever pop the locks?

MAX: Never did. I really wanted to be able to say with conviction, at gunpoint if necessary, that I had no idea what was in your bags. The way you took off, and the way they trashed my house, I figured it had to be money or dope. And I honestly didn't know if you were dead or alive. So when that car pulled up in front of the house in the middle of the night, I started to wish I had crawled through that window, while I had the chance, and disappeared. I was so glad to see you get out of that car, and not some bad guy with blood in his eye. Some heavy with a hard on. Ray.

RAY: I didn't really think you'd be there. Driving across the causeway. Over the ocean, through the Keys. Full moon. I kept thinking. She's gone. And so's the money. I never expected to see you again.

MAX: Takes two to tango, like the song says. I like you, Ray. You've definitely captured my interest. And maybe someday you'll tell me who you really are.

RAY: Maybe.

(They kiss.)

MAX: Your wife?

RAY: My widow.

MAX: Saved your life.

RAY: Hers, too. She had no choice. They would have done everyone. Had she tapped me.

MAX: Still.

RAY: Still. Always was cool. I thought she might lose it when she walked through the door and saw me. Took her by surprise, no question. A bad bad moment. Teetering on the brink.

MAX: I'm not cool. I'm hot.

RAY: Why I like you.

(They kiss.)

MAX: She know you took the money?

RAY: She'll never know. Not for certain.

(Pause)

RAY: I can't even remember who I used to be.

MAX: Neither can I. From here on in we can make it up as we go along.

(They kiss again.)

MAX: Tell me something. Ray. That guy they found in your house? The body? Your ultimate out? Did you kill him?

RAY: No. Swear.

MAX: I believe you.

(Pause. BABCOCK enters, sits near them. They stare at one another for a moment.)

MAX: Oh, shit.

BABCOCK: Coincidence. Really. This time. No kidding. Small world, huh? You're Ray Gaines, right? Or is it Avila?

RAY: Avila. Ray Avila.

BABCOCK: Have it your way. And you're Max, I recall correctly. Short for Margaret.

MAX: That's right.

RAY: Babcock, wasn't it?

BABCOCK: I don't remember.

(Pause)

RAY: I thought you were dead.

BABCOCK: Look who's talking. I made a deal with the guys they sent. The goombahs. We got to shootin' the shit. Passin' the time. They were takin' me out to the Atchafalaya Basin to become part of nature's rich gumbo. Turns out I'm connected. Certain arms merchants. I had some money stashed offshore. A little somethin' for my old age. A rainy day. We made a trade. Money. Weapons. I agreed to leave the country. Change my name. Cease and desist. They agreed not to waste me. Worked out well for everyone.

(He offers his hand.)

BABCOCK: Chibas. Jose Marti Chibas Valenzuela.

(RAY stares at him.)

RAY: Valenzuela. Sounds Cuban.

BABCOCK: As a matter of fact.

RAY: We have to be going now. Don't take offense when I say I hope we never meet again.

BABCOCK: Good luck. Watch your back. You never know what's out there, lurchin' in the dark rapture.

(They look at each other a moment. RAY nods.)

RAY: No. That's right. You never do.

BABCOCK: Thought so. Thought that was you. Lit up
that ville pretty good. Whoosh.

RAY: Quite a night.

BABCOCK: Fuckin' A. Nothin' spookier than a night fire,
huh? Makes you feel so all alone. Cambodia.

RAY: Yeah.

(MAX *takes* RAY's *arm.*)

MAX: Señor Chibas. Have a wonderful new life.

BABCOCK: You too, mi hija. You, too. Vaya con dios.
Hey, Ray. Straight ahead, and strive for tone.

RAY: I'll do that.

(RAY *and* MAX *leave. Babcock leans back in his chair.
Sips his drink.* RENEE *comes on. Gives* BABCOCK *a long
kiss on the mouth.*)

RENEE: Jose. Mi hijo.

BABCOCK: Renee. Mi hija. Want a drink?

(*She sits in the chair beside him.*)

RENEE: Who were you talking to?

BABCOCK: Tourists.

RENEE: Popi? How long are we going to stay here?
I'm bored. Can we go to Mustique? See if Mick Jagger's
hangin' out? We could call him. He's in the book,
you know. He's *listed.*

BABCOCK: Thought we'd leave in the morning.
Go down to Grenada. Spend some time. Look around.
See what we see.

RENEE: Whatever you want, mi amor. Whatever you
want.

(*The lights slow fade to black. The bird and sea sounds
intensify. End of play.*)

www.ingramcontent.com/pod-product-compliance
Lightning Source LLC
Chambersburg PA
CBHW052200090426
42741CB00010B/2344